Teatime

Fashionable New Tea Shops

images
Publishing

Contents

Distinctive tea factories and tea brands

Index

About the author

Zender, lead designer and brand consultant of Heytea, specializes in creative interior design for commercial spaces for young people. After graduation, he worked for seven years at the University of Southern China as a teacher. He spent a great deal of time reading and traveling the world during his vacations, and contributed to National Geographic and Lonely Planet as both a writer and photographer. Later, he was awarded a scholarship from Robert Bosch Stiftung to study at Hamburg University. In 2016, Zender founded his own design studio.

Introduction

Unfinished design

There are sometimes moments in your life where you are suddenly enlightened about your greater potential. For me, meeting Belgian curator Axel Vervoordt in Venice in the summer of 2015 was probably the definitive beginning of a new phase.

The theme of that year's Vervoordt exhibition was PROPORTIO. He reconstructed the interior space of Fortuny Palace, the five stories of which all follow the logic of Sacred Geometry—from the Fibonacci series to Le Corbusier's model theory; decorative art to applied art—showing the role of proportions and systems in art, architecture, and scientific music.

You can easily recognize Vervoordt's great ambition from the span of the works he displayed: Marina Abramovic, the grandmother of behavioral art; Anish Kapoor, a contemporary sculptor, who is famous for his simple lines; Agnes Martin, an abstract painter; and Sol LeWit, an American artist. Together with those famous contemporary artists' works were some Egyptian handicrafts, Japanese Raku teacups, and English farm kitchen cabinets by nameless craftsmen. The collision of these works blurred the boundaries of time and build, a vast, endless, and thought-provoking field.

The artistic inspirations aroused by Axel Vervoordt's exhibition greatly impacted me as a designer. After returning from Hamburg, I was determined to establish my own design studio. I had been trying to find opportunities to execute and complete my own works. Hesitating between settling in Guangzhou,

Shanghai, and Jingdezhen, my entire state could only be described as inexplicably excited, stupid, and irresolute—but very happy.

At that time, Heytea had just entered Shenzhen. It was learned that a large local company had already helped them complete the preliminary design. However, it was obviously not satisfactory in many aspects and a bit too routine. Also at that time, one of my students was working in MULAND, an interior design studio in Shenzhen, which was already on the way to significant innovation and making a breakthrough in the local market. The MULAND team was entrusted with Heytea's interior design.

Through their introduction, I had my first contact with Heytea. In regard to designing a tea shop, even though I try to always maintain an open-minded approach, I was still hesitant and somewhat resistant, but as I didn't have any relevant work experience in China and my studio was only a shell company at that point, I decided to take on the project.

In March 2016, I flew from Shanghai to Shenzhen with a proposal. I had a long talk with Neo, the founder of Heytea, and tasted their impeccable products. In that conversation we discussed how every new generation craves new ideas, and interesting ideas from interesting people. It takes courage to be different. Over our discussion, I sensed the coming of a new era. Countless people had tried to connect young people with the tea culture, yet a new approach was needed. This brought up five questions:

• What is the origin of Heytea as a brand?
• Is the source of tea in Heytea's products different from similar products?
• How could we express the tradition of tea in a fashionable perspective in the new era?
• How could we make Heytea more popular among young people?
• What does this project mean for our design team?

We also considered what a tea shop should look like in the busy marketplace. Tea belongs to a quiet world. It is not a product that can be manipulated through the power of language. So it became very clear that we needed to return to the essence of tea and rebuild everything as though there had never been a tea shop on Earth.

Axel Vervoordt's thoughts on modern art and traditional classics affected my way of thinking. In addition, a sentence from *The Book of Tea*[1] by Kakuzo Okakura, a scholar who influenced the entire Western world in their perception of oriental aesthetics in the 19th century, opened a door for me to solve the problem. He wrote: "Tea ceremony is a kind of worship of incompleteness, and it is a gentle attempt to achieve some possible perfection in an imperfect life that we all know." I then identified the initial key phrase—"Modern Zen."

The Heytea Central Walk Store offered the first concentrated display of "Modern Zen." The design team arranged a special space for the display and performance of the concept of "handmade tea." All custom-made tea prepared by experienced craftsmen from Jingdezhen and Taipei are showed here too. The long strip-shaped table in this handmade-tea experience area is large enough for tea specialists to serve tea to customers one on one.

At the same time, we always try our best to keep the original structure of the space, remove excessive pretentious decoration, and even expose the original structural space if possible. We usually choose a large number of essentially purer materials such as plain cement furniture, stainless steel, cast iron, and terrazzo. The traditional tea room seems to have found a completely different language here to express its style. This style was originally established in Heytea Mix (Huifu East Road, Guangzhou), which is complicated in design but extremely simple in effect. It required a complicated work process, but looked very simple. Two years later, it was still pioneering. In the four-story space, the cold and restrained background colors set off the products themselves. Tea wares, with basic geometric shapes made in Jingdezhen, are stacked under the acrylic shade. They are not only artistic installations but also tables for guests to use in the store. The third floor is the reserved

---

1 Kakuzo Okakura, *The Book of Tea*, Shandong Pictorial Publishing House, 2014.

gallery and is becoming a preferred platform for art exhibitions on young local artists.

In terms of graphic design of Heytea, because I've been a reader of English commercial design magazine *Monocle* and Japanese lifestyle magazine *Brutus* for a long time, I was deeply impressed by the retro and mischievous style of Yokohama illustrator Satoshi Hashimoto, and the simple and clear linear paintings of Mr. Noritake. Inspired by their style and works, I had an idea for Heytea's graphic design, which was finally executed by Mr. Tie Xun, an independent illustrator who was far removed from the industry yet I came across him by chance in a pub exhibition. We become partners and good friends. His smart illustrations met Heytea's needs (and become a target of innumerable plagiarists later!).

In the following year, Heytea marched into Shanghai and Beijing and came into the awareness of the whole industry. Naturally, a lot of shops have emerged. One night, when I was lying in bed and scanning my cell phone before going to sleep I saw a photo in the WeChat group of a Heytea project showing a Heytea developer establishing a store in Shenzhen MIxC. I immediately jumped out of bed and returned to my study. Looking back, I think it was sheer luck. There were rumors at that time that Heytea had paid a large amount money for that location as they had their sights set upon the premium luxury-brand neighbors, such as Prada and Coach.

The store position was, in fact, actually very awkward—it is not the main entrance of the mall, it's relatively independent, and it is even disconnected to the mall internally. Moreover, the café that operated there previously had experienced poor success. The photo in my WeChat showed that the team had stuck to the plain cement style and the whole construction was almost finished. But a bold idea struck me that we needed to create a different type of store that could fit in the different levels of commercial systems, and continuously provide a fresh experience for consumers.

That night I told Neo (the founder of Heytea) that we needed to build a "Heytea Black" in Shenzhen MIXC Mall. We decided to use black cast iron, brass, glass, and furniture and lamps made of volcanic stone to establish a new space integrated with the brand's "Modern Zen."

This story is not over yet. Later, we finished Heytea Mix (Huifu East Road) and MixC Heytea Pink, becoming an exporter of brand values. As this time, my initial contract with Heytea was about to expire. While taking pride in being a participant, I felt a sense of loss. Heytea was already an independent child with growing wings, so would it still need a brand consultant and fashionable design?

When I was on vacation in New York in the spring of 2017, Neo sent a message to me asking if I wanted to continue to work with him and Heytea—I didn't hesitate to say yes! I firmly believed that this rapidly growing brand had only just begun its journey.

When I lived near Chelsea Market in New York, I spent the mornings in various galleries and museums, and the afternoons in a café called Untitled at The Whitney (located at the first floor of Whitney Museum) preparing my design work. It took only a few days for me to have a complete annual plan. That day, I sent the plan back to China from the café. As usual, the team at Heytea gave me instructions to implement it quickly. The plan was for the Daydream Project (DP), which later shocked the whole industry. In the hearts of Chinese people, poetry, wine, fields, mountains, and lakes have always been close to their hearts. Integrated in life, they help people temporarily escape the daily toil and soothe their souls. Art and design have always been a distinctive part of Heytea's genes. So we encouraged many local young artists to display their works in Heytea's shops. In return, Heytea was also willing to share the exciting artistic works with its consumers. DP is a cross-border cooperation between Heytea and independent designers all around the world, from design, peripheral products to retail cooperation. This project seeks to present more designers, brands, and their products with the same spirit of Heytea to all customers.

The first collaborator of DP was my friend, Yan Junjie, an architect who graduated from Central Academy of Fine Arts and Technische Universiteit Delft in the Netherlands, and then worked in top European architectural design companies for six years, including OMA of the Netherlands, Christian Kerez of Switzerland, and BIG (Bjarke Ingels Group) of Denmark. When Yan Junjie returned to China two years ago, we had a short and pleasant conversation in the studio of a mutual friend. On that day, he showed me some pictures of the projects he participated in during his internship at Christian Kerez, which greatly aroused my interest. Rather than trying to pursue the beauty of the form of architecture like many popular architects today, the architectures of Christian Kerez—with a low-key appearance—retains a different understanding of the inherent nature of architecture and its architects: it is an exploration or an experiment. I invited Yan Junjie to take part in DP and we discussed our ideas, which led to the introduction of the systematic thinking of architecture into a commercial dining space.

We made a breakthrough within two weeks. Nowadays, the importance of social networks can never be underestimated, so retail space has a more significant social value than just the goods sold. Returning to the social attributes of the crowd, we can experience their sensual enjoyment. Beautiful details in a shop can bring unique experiences in the senses of spirit, vision, and taste. Therefore, we decided on a change of perception from just a tea shop to a social space as the core concept.

At the Heytea DP (Uniwalk), we put together 19 tables of different sizes into a large table that shortens the distance between different groups—

Below: Heytea DP (Unicenter, Shenzhen)
Photography: Huang Miangui

Below: Heytea DP (Upperhills)
Photography: Huang Miangui

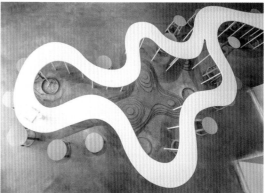

people can sit face to face, back to back, or in a circle. Different ways of sitting can happen in the same large space with coexisting privacy and openness, allowing consumers to gain different space experiences every time they enter the store, and providing them with a possibility of interaction. In Heytea DP (Upperhills), the same logic was applied to make a modern interpretation of "Qu Shui Liu Shang"—the ancients place a "Shang," which is a kind of wine container, with wine in the stream. The Shang slowly floats down along the stream. When it stops, the people facing it have to improvise a poem and drink the wine. People sit around the water, making tea with their guests, chanting poems or painting. In view of the layout of the site space, it was decided that the tables should be scattered around and arranged like "a river" with graceful curves.

In March 2017, I took my team on a tour to Nujiang basin in western Yunnan, China. The grand Nujiang canyon, 196 miles (315 kilometers) long, and squeezed between the Gaoligang Mountain and Biluo Mountain ranges, is probably one of the most remote and magnificent geographical areas in Asia. Possibly because I was used to traveling in my early years, rather than pursuing success and fame judged by mainstream values, I prefer to learn in person about the ways everyday people live, talk, and exist in different places. The trips have always convinced me that treasures are often hidden in the most inconspicuous places. The fun of incense

burning, flower arranging, and preaching inside a house are nowhere near to that of going to real fields and mountains to be nourished by the wind and earth.

That night we stayed in a village in the middle of the canyon. The next day we found a tea garden in the cloud sea where Lisu villagers were picking spring tea leaves. I don't think I will ever forget the tea garden shrouded in cloud and mist and the taste of that spring tea on the tip of my tongue later that day when we walked to the more faraway tea factory.

China is the largest tea-growing country in the world, and Yunnan is also a big tea-growing province, particularly known for the white tea of Jinggu and the renowned Pu'er tea in the south. In the early years, people here lagged behind in terms of farming techniques, and after many years of tortuous exploration, it has developed into the current scale. Tea-picking season begins from the Tomb Sweeping Day (in April) and ends in the middle of November. The tea farms dry the collected tea leaves in the night of the same day, deactivating enzymes, rolling, frying, and then manually screening them.

After the concept and the space design of the first batch of shops were finished, Heytea entered a relatively stable period. At that time, I was thinking about studying the tea industry to see if there were any points for making a breakthrough in the trade

Shenzhen Yili Tea Industry, a supplier of raw materials of Heytea, entered our sights at that time. They had been in the industry for 10 years. Ten years ago, when ordinary raw material manufacturers were still selling some low-priced and low-grade tea dregs, they had begun to provide the top-quality, freshest tea leaves, which had gone through rigorous quality inspection. Now, its average annual amount of processed tea leaves exceeds 3,500 tons. Later, we created a new tea brand together: Jack 2 Tea. The goal was to present all kinds of tea-drink flavors, original and mischievous, and discuss with young people the origin of tea, the customs behind a cup of tea, and the story sewn together by it.

The debut of Jack 2 Tea was at the 27th Shanghai International Hotel and Restaurant Fair (Hotelex) in 2018. In my early research, I discovered that many of the leaders in the coffee industry actually wanted to intervene in the market of the Chinese mainland through this fair in the early years, including Five Elephants from Berlin, Urban Coffee Roster from Hong Kong, and Fritz Coffee Company from Seoul, all of which are regular participants of the fair. These coffee brands have their own systems for the export of their products, design, and values.

Unfortunately, this information was only spread in a small circle and was drowned in the wealth of information at the fair. We thought about what kind of design was needed for the large number of people moving in and out on this site.

chain that provided services for commercial tea-drinking spaces. The selection of the variety, field management, post-processing, baking, and brewing used to be the work of elderly farmers. Now, could we touch the earth to try, experiment, share, and continuously absorb new knowledge?

In combination with the keynote of the brand, the design direction of Jack 2 Tea became clear. We used a bold single color—white. In the center of the venue were two long tables similar to the lines of balance beams. Tea leaves were placed in the most eye-catching position according to the display method of museum exhibits. A slogan was written on Chinese art paper with a brush pen and hung in the tea-making area, becoming the finishing touch. During the days of the fair, I saw numerous visitors go around to take photos of this calligraphy work.

We bought white balloon flowers, big leaf white roses, and grayish green eucalyptus, which we personally arranged into bouquets, and placed them in tea canisters. This detail was actually intended to send a message that the glass tea canisters we specially designed could also be re-purposed as flower vases after being emptied. In my opinion, any small detail is the cornerstone of the brand.

In fact, I have searched for the inspiration for tea all over the world during my work and even in my spare time. Seiji Yamamoto, a Japanese chef, embarked on a journey of world-class cuisine when he was very young. After finishing his studies at a culinary school, Yamamoto spent 11 years in a famous Kaiseki restaurant in Tokyo and mastered Japanese cuisine skills. In December 2003, the 33-year-old chef opened his first restaurant, Nihonryori RyuGin, in Tokyo, which was rated as a Michelin 3-star restaurant because of his creative methods and innovative interpretation of Japanese cuisine.

Nihonryori RyuGin opened in Taipei in 2014. To enjoy its highly praised food, I reserved seats for dinner half a month before my trip to Taipei. In Taipei, a city full of delicious food, I was not sure whether it was worthwhile to dress up and wait for a Japanese dinner. I hoped to find the answer. The restaurant is located at the fifth floor of a modern building. The design uses a lot of stones and wood, and most of stones remain rustic. In addition to the elegant taste of the meal, what was unexpected was the Chinese tea served, which refreshed my perception of tea. After an in-depth study of the characteristics of Taiwan tea, the restaurant selected 20 types of tea (90% from Taiwan) and served tea drinks with

the meals according to the season and cuisine. For instance, the aperitif was replaced with tea juice infused with nitrogen, followed by pressed tea made from orange peel and Taichung oolong; with sashimi comes the grayish-white rock tea from the south of Hengdong peninsula. Finally came a dark black tea that had been aged to pair with meat.

The masterful use of tea drinks led me to notice more pioneering explorations around the world. Samovar, for instance, in San Francisco has long been a supplier of Blue Bottle Coffee. According to local delicacies, they have made a variety of classic table teas, such as nutty green tea and barley tea.

Steven Smith Teamaker of Portland supplies high-quality tea products to many local restaurants. They have introduced a delicious ice-cream made of oolong tea, jasmine, vanilla, and almond. In Japan, the Sakurai Japanese Tea Experience, which is run by Mr. Shinya Sakurai, has become a must-go-to place for my visits to Japan.

Apart from the simple demand for tea polyphenols and caffeine in tea leaves, tea is a medium that can attract all kinds of people and encourage emotional interaction. Western consuming culture has brought influence to the position of tea in young people's hearts, while in the East, people have a natural thirst for tea. Tea can be elegant in a life of lute-playing, chess, calligraphy, and painting, or it can be simple in a life of firewood, rice, cooking oil, and salt. However, living in

the present, we continue to proceed toward the future, break the existing patterns, and continuously explore and innovate.

In the former monastery institution of Zen, all the monks and nuns (apart from the abbot) had to undertake the daily affairs of the whole temple. The disciples with the lowest status were responsible for relatively easy tasks, while the senior brothers with the highest self-cultivation and highest status had to do the most boring and lowly work. Engaging in daily tasks was part of the institution discipline, and even the most insignificant details require

perfection. As a result, many discussions and dialogues that play a decisive role in Zen studies, in reality, began in the weeding in the garden, washing of vegetables in the kitchen, or pouring of tea to serve the masters. From a Zen life that is as light as a feather, people can find a concept heavier than Mount Tai. It can also be said that Zen is the central idea of the entire tea ceremony.

Those who try to progress towards perfection must also be able to maintain their individuality in their daily life, not following trends but discovering the radiance from the inside.

Case Studies

Rabbit Hole Organic Tea Bar

Matt Woods Design Ltd.

Location	Area	Completion	Photography
Sydney, Australia	160 square meters	2015	Dave Wheeler

Matt Woods Design reinvented the tired and clichéd teahouse concept with the Rabbit Hole Organic Tea Bar. The design began by taking advantage of the former industrial site's inherent architecture. Concrete floors were polished; herringbone strutted timber ceilings were unearthed; original brick walls were revealed. The softening of this masculine architecture was achieved through the white-washing of these newly exposed elements, and through the addition of enlarged northeast-facing windows, which allowed light to flood into the interior.

The Japanese art of Kintsugi (which means to join with gold, and is a celebration of the beauty of imperfection in ceramic objects) formed the foundation of the new design elements. This was most apparent in the specialty tea display where, like spinning plates on top of a circus performer's pole, custom-designed Kintsugi bowls sit delicately above turned oak timbers. This precarious balancing act makes the suggestion as to why these bowls required their gold-laden repair job in the first place.

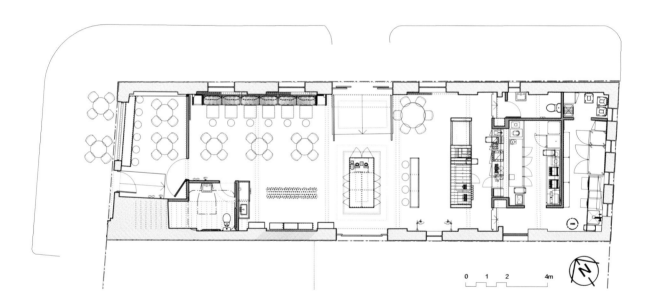

The Kintsugi concept was further reinforced with the expansive use of a crushed ceramic tile, which is featured on the service-dominated areas of the café, such as the central monolithic retail display. The designer made great efforts to ensure that any new feature elements did not get bogged down in non-concept complexity, and above this tile-clad monolith, a chandelier made entirely of tea bags (by Chilean artist Valeria Burgoa) was installed.

To counteract these highly conceptual feature elements, much of the remainder of the design

is more humble in form, yet in no way modest in design detail. A steel-framed glazed wall complete with custom-designed pivoting windows delineates the smaller entry section, which has its own unique, yet complimentary, Mad Hatter aesthetic. Reclaimed-oak timbers create banquette seats and table frames. These were wire brushed, gently oiled, and express dowel joined to reinforce the quality of the design.

A combination of leathers and upholstery fabrics create seat cushions and brass-buckled back rests.

Century-old French-oak floor joists were used to create the service counter, while a shark-nosed granite top sits effortlessly in the room as a group dining table. Other tables are less ostentatious, and were constructed in timber and fiber cement. This contrasting materiality was peppered throughout the space, with $100 warehouse shelving stand alongside and instep with bespoke joinery items.

Further efforts were made to ensure the environmental comfort of all patrons, and perorated E0 custom wood panels conceal acoustic wall linings. Sustainability is at the heart of every design decision, with dematerialization being a key-driving factor. All timbers are either FSC certified or recycled; all paint finishes are VOC free; the lighting is energy efficient or LED. Every material was assessed for its embodied water and energy content. Further to this, the project aimed to eliminate the need for air-conditioning and sought to take advantage of the natural and passive cross-ventilation opportunities on offer.

El TÉ—Casa de Chás

Gustavo Sbardelotto / Sbardelotto Arquitetura, Mariana Bogarin

Location	Area	Completion	Photography
Porto Alegre, Brazil	63 square meters	2013	Marcelo Donadussi

Located in one of the most important commercial galleries in the city of Porto Alegre, El TÉ—Casa de Chás focused on the sale of teas and everything tea related.

The project concept was born from an immersion into the world of teas, with all its colors, textures, and aromas providing the starting point for creating the environment. Wood was selected as the primary material of the space, acting as a neutral base to backdrop the colorful product range.

Due to the shop window being visually obstructed by the wall of the shop next door and also being quite far from the sidewalk, the store needed a strong visual element that would arouse the interest of those who passed by. For that reason, the designers sought a synergy between the elements of visual communication and architecture.

From the graphical representation of the store name—"El TÉ" which literally means "The tea"—the designers developed a pictogram for the teahouse

CLASSIC BLACK · QI MEN · CLASSIC EARL GREY · COCOA · INDIAN FLAVOR · MADRID · BEAM ME UP · EVE · WINTERLY · SENCHA DECAF · HUANG SHAN MAO FENG · JAPAN ESSENCE · VERANO · STRAWBERRY CHAMPAGNE · JADE FLOW

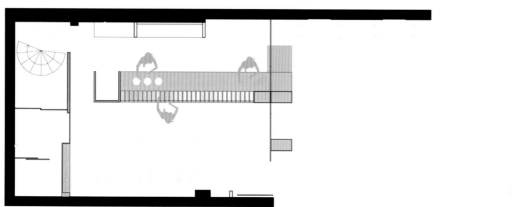

acting as both a visual communication and the main piece of furniture. This went beyond the scale of the usual sign composing the façade and interior design of a shop.

On the façade, "TÉ," which faced the street, the backlighting functioned as an urban lantern and an exciting surprise for those who pass by the store by night. The depth of the letter "É" on the façade extended beyond the outer limit, penetrating inside

the store and acted as the main design element. This element housed the display of teas, the tea-mixing counter, and the cashier counter. The samples of 30 variations of teas were arranged in small drawers so that clients could smell the products before they decided which one they wanted to buy. The 30 variations of the infusions were indicated by different colors beneath each small drawer, which facilitated the identification of each tea by customers and created a colorful scheme.

Gen Sou En Tea House

Suzumori Architecture PLLC

Location	Area	Completion	Photography
Brookline, USA	697 square meters	2018	Shuji Suzumori

The design of Gen Sou En Tea House was inspired by the Gen Sou En philosophy of blending tea and culture, a motif that was realized in the form of geometries, materials, and spatial organization.

The teahouse's programmatic elements were nestled into gently ascending circular forms, whose clean lines reflect modern takes on traditional Japanese architectural features: tatami benches, horigotatsu (recessed seating), a tea ceremony room, and the central Nakaniwa garden, where a tree, moss, and grass grow beneath a hooded circular skylight. The ascending circular forms, which start out as low benches at the front and eventually become full height rooms in the back, when viewed together from the entry, compress the space to make it seem intimate and welcoming, while the same elements together with the linear wood ceiling fins help to expand the space when experienced from within.

The furniture and lighting selection represents the blending of cultures, whether it is a modern Japanese chair inspired by the traditional

Windsor chair or a modern Italian glass light fixture inspired from traditional Japanese lights. The natural walnut, beech, and charred-wood material palette was offset with brass, tatami, Japanese stucco, and exposed, weathered brick, blending the architectural language of traditional and contemporary Japan with a uniquely Boston character. The circular tea ceremony room was finished with Japanese plaster, and some old bricks from the building are revealed inside this room.

The spatial organization was drawn from the Japanese machiya row house typology, where an internal courtyard separates the commercial space in the front from the private dwelling area in the back. The central Nakaniwa garden is not only the focal point of the teahouse with a live, lush, curated greenery under natural light, but also the air of separation between the tranquil lounging area in the back and the busy and active atmosphere in the front.

Biju Bubble Tea Room

Gundry & Ducker Architecture Ltd.

Location	Area	Completion	Photography
London, UK	45 square meters	2014	Hufton & Crow

Biju bubble tea is a tea-based milk or fruit drink with chewy toppings, originating in Korea, which is popular across Southeast Asia. Biju wanted to create a UK-based bubble tea brand to appeal to a discerning London audience, emphasizing quality and taste.

Envisaged as a 21st century tea room, the design emphasized the social aspects of drinking tea. As the shop operates both as a takeaway and also as a social place to come and meet friends, rather than conventional seating such as tables and chairs,

the designers created an internal landscape that people can occupy as they choose. The stepped seating areas allow for group to congregate as well as providing places for people to sit alone. The shop is open until late at night and is a popular place for young Londoners to meet.

At the center of the room is the preparation kitchen. Inspired by a cocktail bar, the idea was to display the raw materials that go together to make the tea and celebrate the theatre of the preparation of the tea. On the counter in a display box is where the

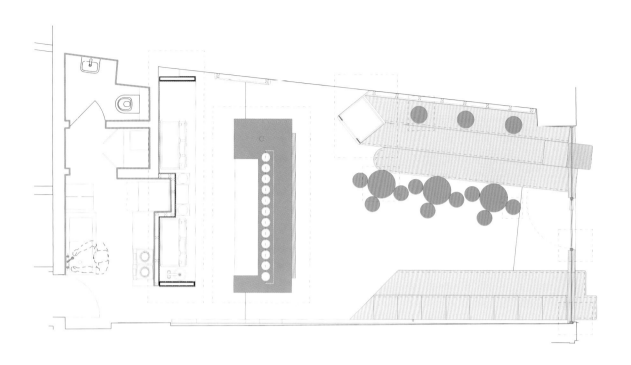

toppings are displayed, and the syrups are displayed on the rear shelf. The tea is dispensed from special dispensers mounted on the wall and prepared in front of the customer.

The use of natural cork in the interior refers to Biju's use of only fresh natural ingredients, whilst the fun aspect of the drinks is reflected by the vibrant colors, neon lighting, and op-art graphics. The graphic stripes that form the Biju branding appear in various forms as painted surfaces, cutting into the plaster finish to reveal the bricks behind and also as neon stripes that illuminate the room.

Screens were incorporated into the seating design, which are regularly updated with social media messaging. Bespoke tables and stools were designed with colorful tops and tubular chrome bases. Small tables were included in the stepped seating. These are flexible, they fit into slots and can easily be removed in the evenings when the shop becomes busy.

Milk. Black. Lemon.

Ryusuke Nanki / Dentsu

Location
Tokyo, Japan

Area
143 square meters

Completion
2017

Photography
Junpei Kato

This concept store was launched by Kirin Gogo no Kocha, one of Japan's leading black tea brands. In contrast to the world of coffee, where there seems to be a constant stream of new concepts, not much happens in the world of tea. This shop was designed as a place to start making black tea news.

In order to create a novel space completely different from the typical chic, subdued tea salon, the designer turned to tea as the inspiration for all aspects of the design. The colors used in the classic herringbone flooring represent black tea and tea with milk. The potted plants are tea trees, the chairs were upholstered in leather the color of tea with milk and tea with lemon, and the other furniture and finishes also feature a tea-inspired palette.

The red color for the wall was taken directly from Kirin's tea packaging, while the cushions were dyed with three types of black tea leaves. The tea lights in the seating area use Japan's world-class food modeling technology to meticulously recreate the many variations on black tea served at the shop, including carbonated tea drinks, fruit tea drinks,

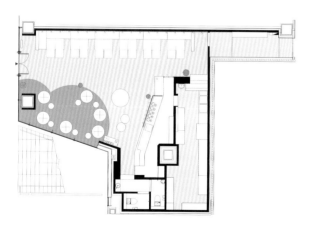

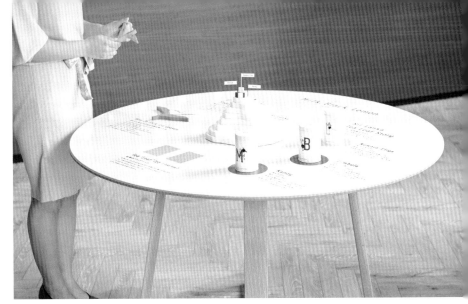

layered teas, and of course tea brewed from various leaves. The teahouse is literally illuminated by the many colors of black tea. The tea-server area features similar models of tea attached at even intervals to a glass wall. On the far side of the glass sit servers filled with multiple shades of black tea, including the three types of iced tea that are the basis for other drinks on the menu, and tea punch infused with fruit. This area functions as a showcase for presenting new styles of black tea.

Nothing in the shop—including the hanging chairs in shades of milk and milk-tea—resembles what one might find in a typical tea salon, but everything is inspired by tea. In addition to the interior design, the designer handled everything from staffing and food design concepts to selection of tableware and other items, going well beyond the typical role of designer. It all came together to offer a relaxing new kind of black tea experience.

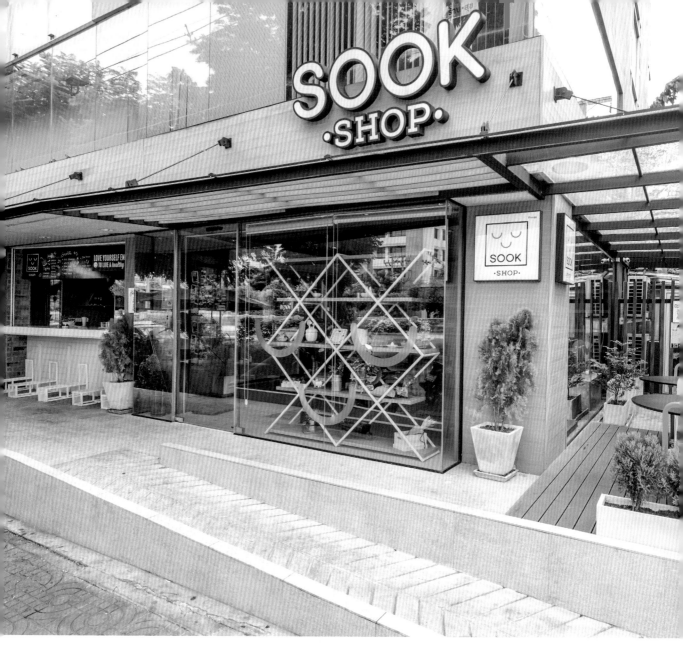

Sook Shop

k2design

Location	Area	Completion	Photography
Bangkok, Thailand	100 square meters	2015	Asit Maneesarn

Located in a peaceful part of the city on Sothern Road, Sook Shop was created for Thai Health Promotion Foundation (ThaiHealth) for health-conscious people. Immediately recognizable, its uniqueness made it stand out on the street. At the entrance, the Bike Bar offered service for cyclists without them having to leave their bikes. The shop also offered a shuttle bus service to the health center in the alley.

The concept of this project was to make the Sook Shop a space that promoted ThaiHealth, with drinks and healthy products for sale that encouraged people to pay more attention to their health. As such, good health was the starting point of the approach to the interior design. The triangle of health (body, mind, spirit) was the main concept, which was integrated into a modern style for the new generation to understand what good health is. Because ThaiHealth wanted to communicate a lot of information, the designers sought to create a fun and relaxing atmosphere.

In addition, the décor of the shop emphasized the green, white, and brown color tones that are visually

soothing and subconsciously promote good health. This beautiful atmosphere provided a zoned layout with a variety of spaces, whether reading in a private corner, sitting at a dining table, or relaxing on the outdoor seating. The materials chosen for the furniture were mostly wood. Great attention to detail was given throughout, as the concept of the project—health promotion—was important. As such, the overall result was well executed.

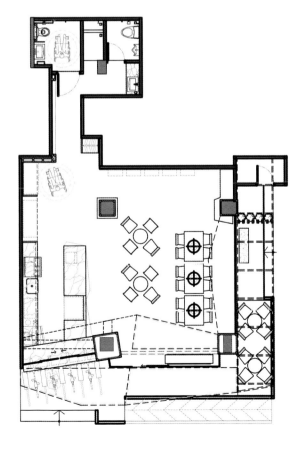

To Tsai

Georges Batzios Architects

Location	Area	Completion	Photography
Athens, Greece	120 square meters	2015	Georges Batzios

To Tsai offers 500 varieties of tea from all over the world. The client requested a unique teahouse: a tea island in the middle of the hardcore center of Athens providing an introverted space with minimalistic architectural details based on the characteristics of traditional Japanese architecture, such as wood, light, and shadows.

An ornament-free, wooden framework occupies the interior skin of the teahouse, which is both functional to display the products and visually pleasing. Form, texture, and function are united under the same distinctive element. Two hundred panels of laminated timber cover the entire interior space in all dimensions in a regular repetitive rhythm that breaks up its regularity periodically while keeping the same rhythm in order to organize the functional areas of the teahouse.

The renovated shop differs from other tea rooms in the area in that—apart from its vast collection of teas—it combines the tea room services with

a retail shop and a light tea-oriented specialty restaurant in the same space. Its visitors are mainly the artsy residents of the area, and even the most-known writers, artists, and journalists of Greece visit To Tsai when looking for a calm space to retreat from this overwhelming area of the city. The ornament-free, minimalistic details of the interior spaces, combined with the wonderful odor palette of the teas and the soft music, create a Zen-like atmosphere for artsy residents and tourist to pause in this noisy part of the city.

The owner originally opened a tea import and retail shop in 1994 just a couple of blocks away from the refurbished shop. He was the first to import high-quality tea in Greece. In 2008, he opened a tea shop in the form of a tea room. Business was slow in the beginning, but since the economic crisis, the business began to boom. Interestingly, when the economy was booming, the tea business in Greece was bad, yet during the crisis, the tea philosophy resonated strongly with the Greek people, as though tea is a natural remedy, which taught

Greeks to adapt to a more minimalistic way of life. This was one good outcome of the crisis, and this is what made the tea philosophy essential to many Greek people. The success of the tea culture is a reflection of the slow change of modern Greek culture away from materialism.

Odette Tea Room

Hugon Kowalski / UGO Architecture

Location	Area	Completion	Photography
Warsaw, Poland	45 square meters	2015	Tom Kurek

Odette is located in the Cosmopolitan, a skyscraper (designed by Helmut Jahn) in Warsaw city center. The project involved creating two areas. The first, with its characteristic plant motif wallpaper, provides a setting with four tables for consuming biscuits and tea—which comes in 100 types from all over the world—while marveling at the historical church in Grzybowski Square. The second area is a red setting that houses the amenities.

The character of the teahouse is emphasized by the original banana-tree-leaves wallpaper, a rosewood counter, veneered tables shaped like leaves, and chairs resembling twig weaves. The plant patterns bring harmony and the gentleness of the plant world into the interior. Standing in stark contrast to the sleek stone plaza, Odette Tea Room offers herbal tea lovers a leafy retreat within the Polish capital's skyscraper district.

Founder of UGO Architecture, architect Hugon Kowalski, infused the base of a tower—referred to as Cosmopolitan Twarda—with a cultivated teahouse characterized by botanical scenery and punctuated

by brass elements. A stone's throw from Grzybowski Square and its historic church, the adjacent plaza filters into the teahouse as a geometric stone floor and wainscot, blurring the shift from outdoor paving to interior flooring. Although the ground changes in a subtle manner, Kowalski's treatment of the walls is another story.

Visitors leave behind the sterility of the encompassing, contemporary cityscape for a tropical scene of lush banana-tree leaves. An asymmetrical grid of brass rods forms a spatial lighting fixture, which visually extends into a matching metal shelving framework. Chrome canisters filled with diverse tea varieties line each shelf.

A rosewood-veneered counter sits alongside circular tables topped with the wood veneer as an inlaid foliage motif are complemented with twig-like legs and chairs.

Cha Le

Leckie Studio Architecture + Design

Location
Vancouver, Canada

Area
63 square meters

Completion
2017

Photography
Ema Peter

Cha Le provides a modernist interpretation of the traditional Chinese tea ritual. The space is defined by a minimalist character that relies on an interplay of geometry and material uniformity. A meticulously coordinated plywood matrix operates as an ordering system for the casework and retail display; this motif is replicated throughout the space to create a sense of rhythm, depth, and shadow. This uniform material backdrop lends visual calm and abstract serenity to the immersive sensual experience of drinking tea.

The focus on wood is economical, and alludes to the sensitivity to materiality that is significant to traditional Chinese tea ceremonies, and often expressed through humble materials. The sculptural mass and quality of the tea bar creates and shapes the space around it, finding inspiration in the Modernist sculptures of Donald Judd, in which materials such as plywood are distilled into their reductionist forms. Cha Le makes use of a restrained quantity and minimal tonal qualities in the materials used, expressed through a uniformity

in the material palette. Whereas the ordering structure of the space may be described as rigid and orthogonal, the architect intentionally softened perceptual hard edges by choosing a warm, light palette that adds a sense of intimacy to the overall experience of the space.

The teahouse adopts a warm and subdued sense of lighting throughout the space. Embedded within the grid, the LED light panels hover in a mysterious manner, blurring over the crisp lines of the grid. Natural light is allowed to filter in through the shop-front, connecting the teahouse to the street-level patio.

Materiality is central to the tea ceremony—beyond the sensual qualities of the tea, the interplay between natural elements in the space and objects of the ceremony equally inform the experience. The ceremony of exchange, and the concentration

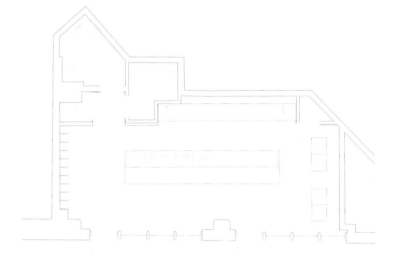

of awareness towards posture and gesture, is articulated through simple objects. The senses are heightened by focusing on a single material, revealing the variations and unique qualities that are inherent to items of ritual. The design for Cha Le interprets this attentiveness by elevating modest, ubiquitous construction materials to allow for architectural clarity and refinement.

Palæo—Primal Gastronomi

Johannes Torpe Studios

Location	Area	Completion	Photography
Copenhagen, Denmark	250 square meters	2015	Johanne Torpe Studios

Inspired by the simplicity of the paleo diet and lifestyle, the design team at Johannes Torpe Studios created an inviting rustic environment for Palæo using raw materials such as leather, wood, and wool. A modular system was designed based on the client's desire to optimize and enhance the workflow behind the counter. The space was additionally designed as a scalable concept to ensure ease of expansion throughout locations of varying sizes.

Palæo—Primal Gastronomi is a healthy concept with a strong focus on fresh and unprocessed produce. They serve tea and coffee and other fresh food, so it's more than just a teahouse. This DNA has been accentuated in the new design and interior concept by Johannes Torpe Studios through the creation of a warm and welcoming universe for their growing customer basis.

The client wanted to create a setting that evoked a feeling of Danish hygge (this Danish

word is an expression dedicated to an innate feeling of coziness that can be achieved through environments and social situations) and homeliness. They wanted to convey that they were more than a takeaway place, and that called for the creation of an interior that entices people to actually stay and hang out.

The new design concept is divided into different areas—accessible seating areas as well as more cozy lounge areas—in order to meet the needs of the wide variety of customer demographics. The feeling of hygge and comfort was achieved through a toned-down color scheme and natural materials such as leather, stone, wood, brass, and wool that create a relaxed ambience in the space.

With locations varying drastically in size—as well as rapidly expanding business—it was of great importance to create a concept with a focus

on scalability. The concept was designed to be easily integrated into various sizes and types of spaces, while still maintaining its identity. This was achieved through the creation of a modular spatial concept, with zones and areas that can be adjusted according to each individual space.

Eshai

Landini Associates

Location	Area	Completion	Photography
Gold Coast, Australia	180 square meters	2016	Ross Honeysett

The tea brand Eshai commissioned Landini Associates to design a two-story tea shop at The Kitchens Robina, a new food mecca on the Gold Coast in Australia.

Eshai is a special tea maker, elevating tea to its art form, inviting customers to a sensory travel into tea cultures from the Far East to Indigenous Australia. One of the most exciting design challenges was working out how to break the mold, move away from cultural clichés, and bring to life a modern shell for traditional tea making.

The overall look and feel was raw and warm with subdued lighting, allying industrial and natural materials such as stone, metal mesh, concrete, and plywood panels. On Level 4, the shop featured a signature element, the Tea Library, displaying from floor to ceiling the tea collections as well as selected accessories from travels around the world. At the heart of the store was a long counter made for tea tasting. The bench included a beautiful brass tap adding a sophisticated spark and a spice palette embedded into the stone to create different tea mixes.

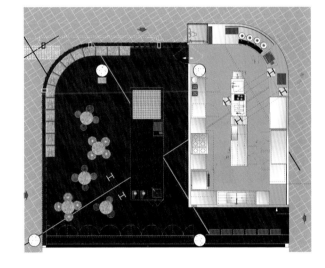

The teahouse offered a multi-sensory journey into a world of flavors, a charming cacophony of colors, fragrances, tastes, and textures. The pared-back beauty of the environment let the food and beverage be the heroes. The transparent kitchen showcased the food-making process, enticing shoppers to step in and activating the takeaway counter. On Level 5, a more intimate and moody space was created for tea ceremonies. Low seating solutions such as tatamis, mats, ottomans, rugs, and beanbags brought a communal, multi-ethnic, and egalitarian feeling.

Jetlag Bar—Tea & Wine

Mimosa architekti

Location	Area	Completion	Photography
Prague, Czech Republic	55 square meters	2017	BoysPlayNice

This small bar in the center of Prague was created to offer tea and wine, as well as coffee, separately or even in various astonishing combinations. The space concept of traveling through time zones was derived from its name "Jetlag." Within this meaning one can "fly through" the entire world along the whole length of the bar (49 feet; 15 meters).

The idea was that the entire world was crammed in there—24 time zones compressed into a few seconds; an utter huddle and muddle. One would enter and within a few steps walk into yesterday.

The design made it so it took six figurative hours to get to the bar end and an additional 13 hours to reach the last table at a window.

The substance of the spatial solution to the Jetlag bar consisted of the idea of "cutting its space into time zones." The curvature of real time zones was generalized in the bar morphology. Each zone began and terminated with a curve delimiting the space part of concern. The shaping of curves created particular parts of the bar space—the bar itself, wine and tea shelves, light fixtures, benches.

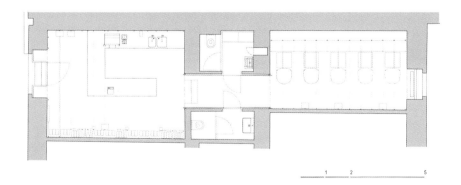

The space was intentionally unclear, as if blurred in the same way as the time in which one travels through distances and time zones.

Stainless steel was chosen as the basic material. The bright, subtle steel curves reflected the imaginary lines delimiting the time zones. The shiny metal associated both the fuselages with riveted sheet metals and the stainless vessels of today's wineries as well.

things i
1. You
2.

Jouri Dessert & Tea

Red5studio

Location
Hanoi, Vietnam

Area
220 square meters

Completion
2016

Photography
Lai Chinh Truc

The site of Jouri Dessert & Tea was an old French villa that was divided in half for rent. Hanoi is one of the most famous coffee shop centers in Vietnam. Due to the cold weather, most of the coffee shops in Hanoi are decorated with deep and warm colors in order to incite a cozy atmosphere.

To stand out in the marketplace, the design team brought a whole new point of view to this cake and bakery shop, wedding an ambient Scandinavian atmosphere with hints of the South Pacific. The young owners, only 23 at the time, wished to create unique and extraordinary space for tea and cake lovers. Therefore, the designers framed the concept based on their favorite quote: "Life is a big adventure."

The space offers a journey across the ocean, using images and materials typically seen on the beach, such as wax wood, decorative items with a lot of images of bottles, cabinets, and chests. What's more, bamboo was used to create a more contemporary design.

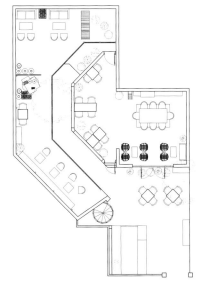

T-Bar

Dos G Arquitectos

Location	Area	Completion	Photography
Panama City, Panama	160 square meters	2016	Pro Pixel Panamá

Originating as a tearoom, over the years T-bar evolved its product range to become a natural-food franchise. As such, they sought to create a fresh look for their new store opening in the banking center of Panama. The new concept had to remain true to the origins of the franchise while also transmitting the new culinary direction; a space where the key elements of the new menu were juxtaposed in the design.

The design team chose to use the same material for both the walls and flooring in order to evoke the sense of the inner courtyards that are so common in the old quarters of Europe. Everything was designed and made out of polished concrete. Walls made of moss and lichen offer the space a striking aesthetic while also affirming the natural theme. Trees were literally built into the tables to form a soothing canopy over customers as they dine.

An array of seating choices were selection to better reflect the moods of customers throughout the day, such as chairs for busy lunches, a padded booth for leisurely breakfasts, and armchairs

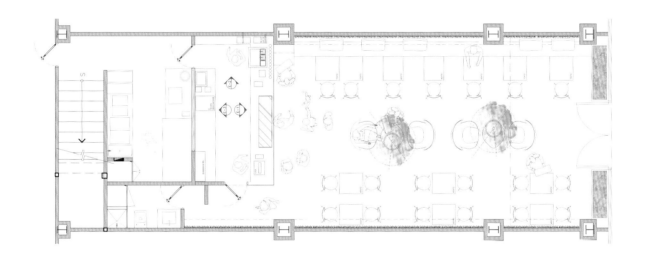

for those seeking a quiet space to work on their laptops as they sip tea.

The designers chose a solid volume of concrete for the serving counter with a metal mesh that offers a translucency while also allowing visibility of the menu. The client requested that the kitchen also be visible to the customers and, as such, it is framed behind a window so that people can see the process of preparing tea.

Heytea DP (Upperhills)

Yan Junjie / A.A.N Architectural Design, MULAND

Location	Area	Completion	Photography
Shenzhen, China	137 square meters	2018	Huang Miangui

It is never too important to underscore social networking today, so retail spaces have social value beyond the goods they sell. The touch of real material can bring about sensuous enjoyment. Only details that inspire a sense of beauty from spirit as well as senses of vision and taste can offer unique experiences. Focusing on the change from a tea store to a social space was the key concept of Heytea store in Upperhills of Shenzhen.

In the hearts of Chinese people, poetry and wine, gardens, mountains and rivers are always with them.

They are the background of real life and can be viewed at a distance or explored closely. They are places for people to rest and enjoy life. The ancients used to put cups brimmed with wine on a stream. The wine cups slowly floated down the meandering water, stopping in front of people, who would have to drink the wine and improvise a poem. Sitting beside a river and flowing cups of wine, making and drinking tea, chanting poems and painting pictures are always romantic activities for ancient scholars and poets.

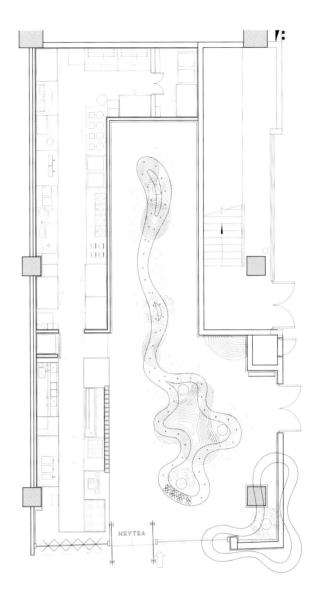

The same logic was used in Heytea (Upperhills, Shenzhen) to give a modern interpretation of "flowing wine cups on winding water" The designers, considering that the space is narrow in the inner interior and spacious in the outer interior, created molded tables in the form of an elegantly winding stream. A large area of water-wave stainless steel spreads over the entire ceiling, which looks look ripples floating in the sky.

TMB concept store

DPD Consultant

Location	**Area**	**Completion**	**Photography**
Guangzhou, China	80 square meters	2018	Yu Bai, Michael Lin

TMB (Tea Mixture Bar) is a casual luxury tea brand, as well as an experimental product of design and commerce.

Cooperating with a fashion select shop, TMB is located in a new business center in Guangzhou, which embodies art, humanism, nature, and shopping. Michael Lin, the project director and co-founder of TMB, tried to show his unlimited art imagination in this limited space. His idea was to use this unique style of the tea product to open the gate of fashion, lead the young generation to the passionate new wave of art and tea.

Living in the society filled with information fragmentation, people are easily lost in rapid changes. The designer wanted to encourage the visitors by visualizing the ever-changing world to see, to touch, to feel the emotional waves of the creator, to taste the rules of changes, and to enrich the color of their lives.

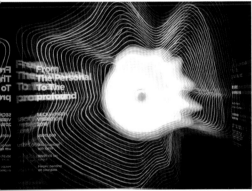

Transforming the abstract art to the appreciable languages of space as well as creating a profit at the same time was the key concept of this design. The designer broke the traditional concept and started from above. He created waves of countless tubes on the ceiling to free the ground; thus, successfully created the Rhythm of Tubes.

The concept of tube waves was not only a simple art expression, but a method to breakdown the original space limit. The project is located at a corner in the mall with very limited usable area. The designer divided the shop into different functions: outside display, dining, bar, art, and product presentation. All of these areas are surrounded by the tubes harmoniously.

The shop is open in an arc shape to welcome the guests. The wavy tubes of many layers are like a mysterious forest, which attracts guests to explore and enjoy. The design of space inversion freed more area in the dining section for customers. Tables of

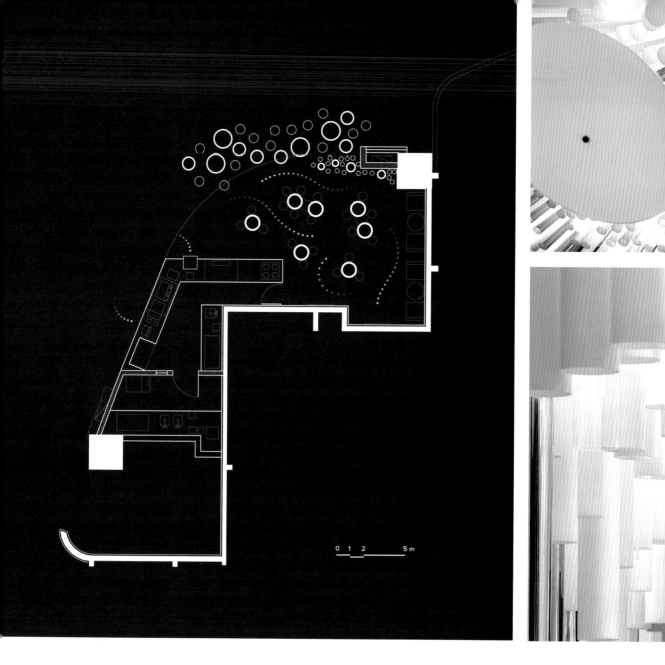

three different heights hanging from the ceiling offer options for customers to sit or stand beside, also making the whole space simple and light.

The designer chose to cover most of the walls with mirrors. With the reflections of the tubes, the limited space is filled with dramatic diversity. Abandoning the traditional layout of a teahouse, the designer put the bar counter in the center of the shop. Customers can witness the whole process of tea making, feel the spirits of the tea masters, and taste the richness of tea.

Black and white were the base of the design, as well as the theme of the brand. The strong contrast of the two colors is just like the signature product of TMB: black as the condensed tea; white as the enriched milk. A mix of different portions can create various adventures for the taste buds. Tea mixing is a self-exploration process. There's no standard

recipe. You can only find your own unique style
through trial and error.

Facing the fierce competition of the tea market,
DPD Consultant managed to balance its roles
between operator and designer. They will continue
to experiment to mix brand-new products with
unique space experiences, and find the piece of
peace in the ever-changing world.

smith&hsu

Divooe Zein Architects

Location	Area	Completion	Photography
Taipei, China	138 square meters	2017	smith&hsu, Divooe Zein Architects

In 2017, smith&hsu invited Divooe Zein Architects to create a new concept shop for them. The new store, as an upgrade of the brand 10 years after its founding, not only continues the original positioning of the brand, but also takes science as the design focus and introduces nature into urban spaces, creating a natural space of unique style for Beijing people who love tea.

The concept of a floating teahouse, as a spiritual window of contemporary teahouses, gives people a strong sense of block-shaped volume; the use of Western modern techniques on lines and materials expresses freedom and creates a sense of depth. The height difference helps create a sense of stability and comfort, which not only isolates the space from outside noises, but also allows you to watch the outside bustling life. The marble round tables and oak square tables in the guest area are interspersed with each other. The handmade paper lamps hang from the ceiling, emitting the warmth of those who crafted them.

Walking inwards, a tea service area with the same floating structure can be seen integrated with the shop-in-shop concept. At the end of the passage is a long horizontal open bar counter and an array of tea-leaf display areas. On the giant copper tea tray, which is handmade using over 30 production processes, are smelling jars purchased by smith&hsu

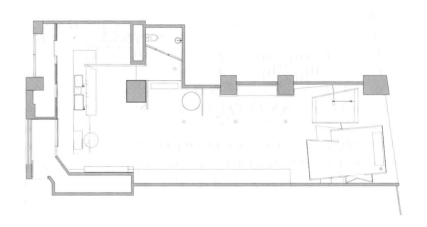

from the East and the West, making the choice of tea-leaf a quite different experience.

Handmade rattan seats present a conflicting and harmonious aesthetic beauty in this contemporary teahouse. Square and round shapes are interspersed throughout the house in different forms, materials and dimensions, and together create a space of rich layers where one can wander around and enjoy the feeling of floating clouds and flowing water.

Since its founding, the smith&hsu brand has been dedicated to creating a new tea experience for a new generation and a place where people can relax at any time, making tea beautiful due to time. The smith&hsu contemporary teahouse developed on this idea, aiming to provide a new experience for stressed urbanites, allows people who enjoy tea here to blend into nature in body and soul and experience a moment of leisure and tranquility.

Heytea Mix (Fuli Haizhu Square)

MULAND

Location	Area	Completion	Photography
Guangzhou, China	240 square meters	2018	Huang Miangui

The whole design aimed to create an introverted and subtle emotional connection with functions of solutions "based on the power of simplicity." To realize such a goal, the space was left with much blankness. The designer only chose terrazzo of light colors, stainless-steel plates, and earth-tone walnut as the main materials, which were dotted with a small amount of brass abstracted into lines.

The highlight of this design was the re-thinking and expression of terrazzo—this common material easily found in the city construction of Guangzhou and in the history of citizens' living—in forms and ways of use. Different from the regular and fine grains mixed inside normal terrazzo, the specially-processed terrazzo consisted of grains of intentionally enlarged sizes customized for this space. The changing of a familiar texture to a strange one was indeed filled with randomness and an intriguing charm.

On the other hand, by placing a large number of stairs made of this kind of material and benches

into the space and removing the traditional setting of seats, people could obtain a casual and loose relationship while seated high or low.

The project was an exploration of the imprint of the past on the city and a clever transition of the history into the poetic aesthetics of space design. Upon people's apprehension of these delicate changes, their connection with the tea also begins.

théATRE TEA (Beijing) concept store

Yen Partnership Architects

Location	Area	Completion	Photography
Beijing, China	128 square meters	2016	Shu He

théATRE TEA offers a contemporary alternative to the traditional tea experience. Believing that tea is ceremonial, communal, and a beautiful ritual, the design team created the first concept store for this completely new tea brand. The space is made for experiencing the beauty of tea mixology, which at the same time is part of the brand spirit.

The first challenge was to filter out the noise and crowd but still create a sense of a place that was a part of office life for everyone in the tower; a place to enjoy and appreciate the beauty of tea on a daily basis. The designers tried to eliminate the visual boundaries as much as possible to make the shop a part of the lobby lounge for the office tower, yet without spreading the seating and tables out to the main lobby area, which is designated for special events only. A physical perimeter closure was still necessary for the extremely dry and cold winters in Beijing. In order to maintain the feeling of openness in the summer, the full-height glazed walls at the shop front are movable panels.

As the brand name suggests, théATRE is a performance space. The bar is the best performance stage for tea mixologists. While waiting for the tea to be made, customers can pick up great selections of the tea in the retail area or enjoy watching the tea mixing and brewing process by the mixologist. The shop signs and brand objects work as the hints for this metaphoric theater space.

The brand also emphasizes the natural aspects of tea. The designers transformed the natural environment into interior design elements, such as the curve of the bar counter from a river and the shape of the custom pendent lights from tea leaves. Modern tea-shaped monograms that resemble tea DNA were engraved at each layer of the glass, creating an interesting optical aligning effect when audiences stand right beneath the pendant; representing the mixology of traditional tea and modern office life.

The ceiling meshes around the pendent lights creating the lighting effect, which resembles the layers, different shades of green in a tea farm on a misty day. The space provides a relaxing

atmosphere for customers to enjoy the great mix of tea. With boundaries reduced, the shop becomes a space open to natural light that shines over the office lobby, with contrasting tones at night. To cater to the changes in natural light, colder light temperatures were implemented on the outskirt of the shop, while the service island and copper back wall were brushed with warmer lights.

The backdrop of the shop is a floor-to-ceiling tea storage wall. The counter was elongated to display the tea-mixing performance, but the tea-mixing process requires roughly 70 tins of tea handy along the bar. Therefore, the back bar and its wall became the best display of the tea available at the store.

The inspiration for the shape of the shelves came from the bamboo basket for tea leaf picking. The bamboo weaving pattern forms the feature wall and function as a tea display at the same time. There is also a tea and spices spinning table available at the counter where orders are placed. The spinning table is the best tool for the customer to experience the richness, beauty, and varieties of tea mixing.

Heytea DP3—Beyond the Mounts, and People Beyond

Yan Junjie / A.A.N Architectural Design, MULAND

Location	Area	Completion	Photography
Guangzhou, China	170 square meters	2018	Zeng Zhe

The third store of the Daydreamer Project series, Heytea sought to explore a new social relationship in the context of the modern era. Continued on from the design concept of the previous two stores, the space was designed experimentally to explore the ways people gather and scatter in the shop. Differing from standard tea shops with seats spread out, the long tea table was positioned through the entire space to make customer aggregation possible.

Additionally, the structures that represent the layering hills in the cloud world, which is a classical scene in the Chinese traditional ink-and-wash paintings, upheave irregularly on the top of the table, and meanwhile, divide the tea drinkers into various sections functionally.

With the white, curved, mountain-like ceiling above, it seems like, with the help of some imagination, customers are placed in the scenario created in the renowned ancient painting, *Auspicious Pines*

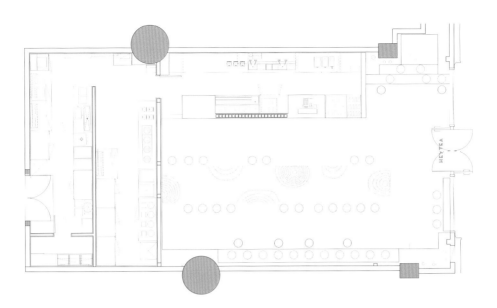

in Spring Mountains by Mi Fu of the Song Dynasty. In the valleys teemed with cloud and mist and mountains shadowed by the greens, a sip of tea is taken on each seat.

This shop was awarded the London Design Award in 2018.

Ruetraa

Tang Zhitao / FZD-Studio

Location	Area	Completion	Photography
Guangzhou, China	195 square meters	2017	Liang Zhanpeng

Throughout the ages, tea has become deeply integrated as one of the emotional exchange carriers among Chinese people. Additionally, with the growing focus on people wanting to live in harmony with nature, the design team applied the form of a tree presented by timber modeling, and created the effect of leaves with artistic chandeliers. In the space, customers would receive the natural ecological concept of returning to one's original simplicity.

The project built upon the logo of Cantonese tea, thereby laying the themes of a black and gold color scheme and concise lines. The visual elements of the Cantonese tea brand were echoed by using black and gold as colors of positive space. Meanwhile, a large quantity of white space and outspread lines exist harmoniously together, which leaves imaginary space and creates visual relaxation for customers, and the concept of happiness is gradually rooted among people.

In addition to experiencing the dynamic rhythm of the music in those fancy bars, people can also better experience Ruetraa. At different periods of

every night, people can enjoy different styles of music—pop, rock, and jazz from the bar bands—while also enjoying the drinks.

The brand concept of "tea plus music equals happiness" was integrated by stage and musical elements. Spatial division was guided by the height proportion of the furniture. The layering of space was improved, and the functional layout division was completed through the combination of a high bar counter, booth, recliner, and outdoor furniture. At the same time, the metal tubes on the wall

echo with the metal tubes on the bar counter, which lowers the district feature brought about by functional division, and makes the whole space more integrated.

The design team chose furniture in a simple and graceful style, the subjective color is roughly similar and echoes with black and gold, the color of positive space through stacking furniture of different types. Based on spatial diversity, the French window at the door serves as both a façade and functional booth. They used a receding technique to revitalize the form

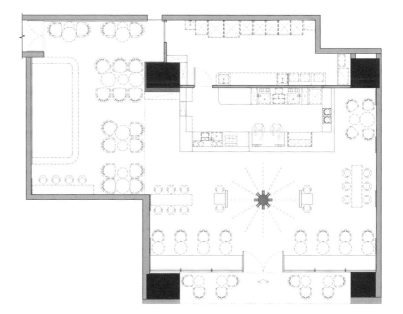

of the French windows; therefore, when it is closed, it could distinguish the outdoor food division and indoor division. When it is open, the party format becomes more diversified with the connecting room.

When making the tree modeling, the designers had to overcome the problems encountered, including the structural mechanics, how to fix it, how to connect the tree structure, and the force problem of the chandelier.

inWE flagship shop (Westgate Mall)

DPD Consultant

Location	Area	Completion	Photography
Shanghai, China	150 square meters	2017	Daqi Cheung @MeeCa photography

The whole space of this flagship tea shop in the Westgate Mall in Shanghai is like a giant open tea box on the busy street, revealing itself to guests seeking a sense of belonging. It's not just a tea shop, but a showcase of a new lifestyle and a window between people and tea culture.

For most young people, the obstacles preventing them from falling in love with tea culture are the ritualistic procedure, complicated making process, and the old-fashioned teahouse design.

Tea is stereotyped as complicated, serious, and traditional, but actually it can be different. DPD Consultant was commissioned by inWE to design the store to present traditional Chinese tea culture through a modern design method, refreshing young people's opinion and creating a natural, attractive place to buy and drink tea.

Wooden gratings showing windows, open seating areas, and bright, neat indoor space make the whole tea shop stand out in the hustle and bustle

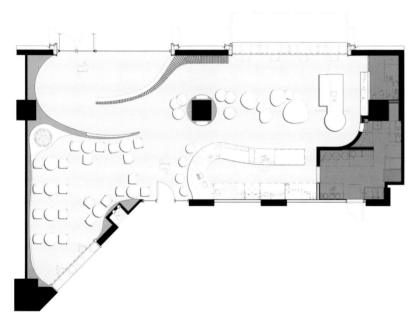
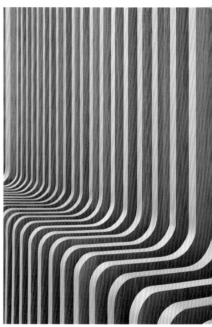

of the street. Customers can enjoy the urban view through the windows while drinking tea. They can rest, chat, and people-watch.

To encourage the young generation to embrace traditional tea culture, the designers sought to change the cultural context and communication style. DPD Consultant fused the symbolizing element from traditional tea culture with the inWE brand. A large amount of the circulation design

originated from the idea of ripples in water. The round celling was inspired by the patio in traditional architecture, intending to create a cozy atmosphere. Additionally, the color scheme chosen was neutral to offer customers a more relaxing environment.

Studying behavioral and psychological pattern of customers in a space is crucial for improving space usage and increasing business value. In this project, the designers set up multifunctional divisions to

meet different customers' needs. For example, the consulates in the surrounding area bring a lot of drop-by consumers, so the designers created a side bar and an express zone to offer quick service.

The product display area next to the open show window gives pedestrians a quick view of the shop. At the long bar, people are encouraged to taste different tea leaves and share in the tea-making process. The round water stone wall is for displaying

photos. In other areas, customers can feel the beauty of tea from different aspects. Customers get to see and smell the products in their own way.

Every little detail about tea culture evolved into a concrete shape to be integrated into people's daily lives. DPD Consultant optimized the visual system for customers, unified the space and brand, and offered a better material supply system for the shop.

Heytea Mix (Huifu East Road)

MULAND

Location	Area	Completion	Photography
Guangzhou, China	105 square meters	2016	Huang Miangui

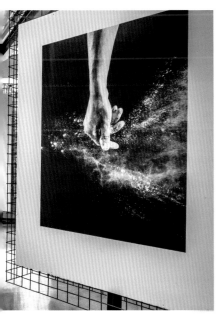

The site on Huifu East Road in Guangzhou was the first commercial display space for the Heytea baking brand, Heytea Mix. This street integrates culture, entertainment, and commerce in Yuexiu District of Guangzhou City. As such, it was an ideal place in the mind of the founder to open Heytea Mix to "give back to neighbors." Heytea is rooted in community and developed in it, therefore, this project also takes "community" as its creation concept.

The space that was designed based on these concepts reveals a natural and low-key minimalist core in its combination of materials such as cement, walnut wood, black iron, and stainless steel. The individual building was originally an old urban house, a three-story structure that provided room for creating a space with rich texture.

The design strategy was to maximize the use of the spatial characteristics of the old house, and skillfully integrate the three-story indoor space with complex and diverse business activities on the street, thus creating a subtle, lively and interesting multidimensional street and lane space. In view of

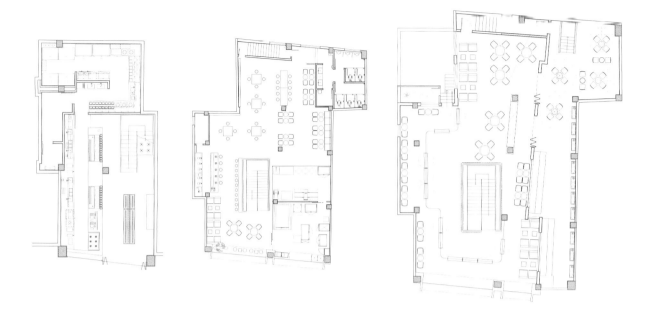

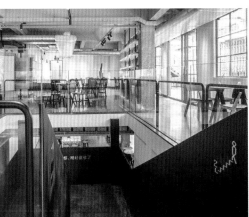

the characteristics of its business district, the design departs from the spatial form of a traditional single business model and gives this space more cultural, artistic, and public content.

The first floor is the central sales area of tea drinks and bread; the second floor is for bread baking, the whole process of which can be seen through glass. The production of all bakery products must be completed in the store, and the whole process from on-site dough-kneading and molding to baking can be done in the baking room. Bakery products are for sales on the same day and not delivered to other stores.

The third floor is an art space that provides artists with the opportunity to display their works occasionally. The three tiers of space are staggered over each other, creating an immersive multi-dimensional sensory experience for customers.

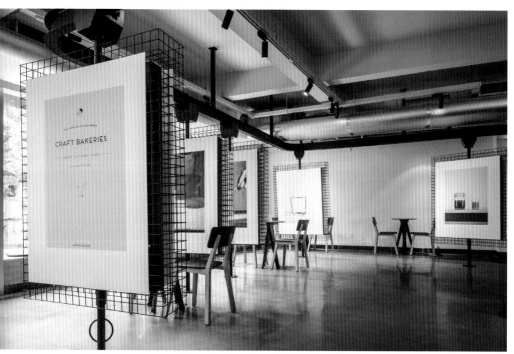

Teasure

Young H Design

Location	Area	Completion	Photography
Xi'an, China	250 square meters	2016	Lentoo Studio

Tea is a traditional drink for Chinese people and this brand is devoted to the promotion of modern tea. Different from most tea shops that flourish on the street, there is one more like Starbucks in the tea industry: Teasure.

The Teasure brand invited a Japanese design master, Kenyahara, to create the visual image of the company. Young H Design was honored to participate in the design of the store. The entire space is dominantly minimalism, free of excessive decoration. The design concept defines the tea bar as a "cup of tea." The designers created a bright atmosphere unlike what is normally found in dim ordinary cafés and bars. The bright tones make it easier for people to clearly see the color of the tea.

All decorations were chosen based on the "beauty of tea." Screens with ink paintings in ancient-style contrast with modern furniture; blackboards displays the traditional tea ceremony to young people through vivid stick drawings; the wooden bar and ordering cards in a craft-like shade echo well with warm-toned wood, as well as dining

tables and floors made of wood. All of these elements create a homely atmosphere. The wallpaper of the primary wall is decorated with tea-leaf patterns. It can be said that tea culture is integrated everywhere in the store, creating a tea space worthy of the name.

To achieve the brand purpose of Teasure, the designers created a small and beautiful store. In this tea-filled space, busy modern people can find a small area for relaxation while also immersing themselves in tea culture and enjoying a very pure tea experience.

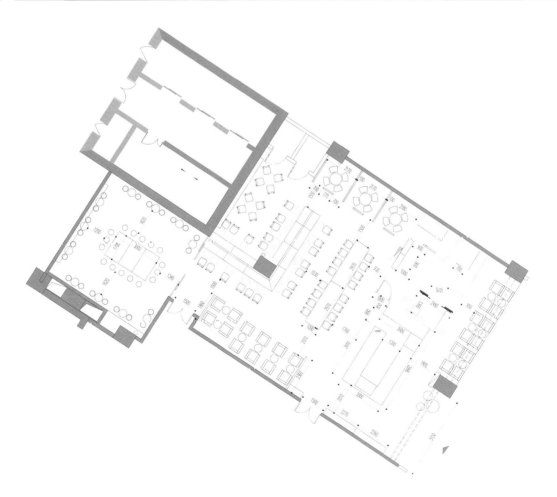

Hi-pop Tea concept store

Construction Union

Location	Area	Completion	Photography
Foshan, China	50 square meters	2016	Ouyang Yun

This project is located in an old street full of nostalgia. It is called CD Street—a place filled with CDs, toys, and elaborate works. No longer bustling as it once was, in this fast-developing era of booming buildings, streets of old neighborhoods such as these are quietly slowing down. But the memories never die.

The project for this trendy brand drink store was to target a demographic of mainly fashionable youths. The designers' first idea was to build a fashion store to lead the tide of fashion of this old street through integrating old memories into the store.

The designers, at the same time, wanted to combine Hi-pop's brand concept to upgrade the store image through design, so as to increase its social awareness in the long term.

The design concept was derived from the delicious childhood pleasure of drinking carbonated soft drink through straws. The indoor space of the site is a rectangle built mainly by connecting two space blocks—a yellow box and a black box. The ceiling was decorated with straw elements that extend from the entry to the deepest interior space and

connect the yellow box and black box. It reaches the deepest parts of the space, just like the burst of taste and texture when we drink soft drinks.

Blocks of the floor and wall use encaustic tiles with sketches, reminiscent of school days doodling circles on paper during boring classes. The combination of the two blocks and ceiling, and the interweaving of spaces, together with the decoration of simple but strange monster and fashionable doll designs seeks to evoke customers' memories of their childhoods. The whole atmosphere is uplifting while also encouraging a fast dining experience to increase turnover. Such a design fits the business operating mode of today's fashionable food and beverage space.

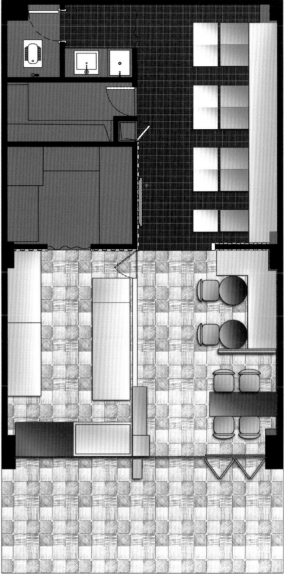

Heytea (Suzhou)

MULAND

Location	Area	Completion	Photography
Suzhou, China	309 square meters	2017	Huang Miangui

Chinese classical gardens have always been known as "literati gardens," many of which gather in Suzhou. To keep with the times and adopt a proper ancient style, the spirit of innovation was rooted in traditional Chinese gardens, and Heytea (Suzhou) is a study and tribute to the landscape architecture of traditional gardens.

The most remarkable features of Chinese gardens are rockery, flowers and trees, and open windows and doors in garden buildings and walls. The designers divided the new store space by exquisite border frames, and built a cubical pavilion. These like picture frames, frame the opposite close view, thus slowing down the pace of walking and creating interest. The space is expanded invisibly, and the scenery is brought in through open windows and doors, thus the real scenery turns into a virtual world in the mind of tea guests, creating endless fun.

The mountains are clothed in trees and the trees have mountains as their bones. An appropriate number of trees can show the beauty of mountains,

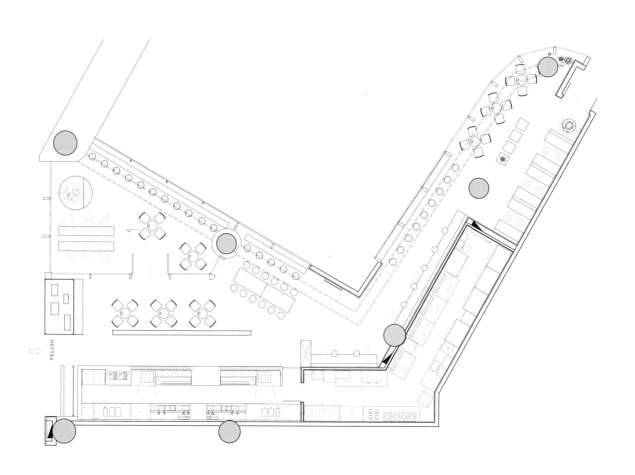

and a neat mountain can set off the luxuriance of trees. The designers placed beautiful flowers and plants on outdoor and indoor long tables. When tea guests run their eyes over the smartly arranged flowers and trees, they will find one more layer between their sight and the scenery, which gives them a sense of concealment and depth. You can walk or stop in these tearooms, enjoying different views along the way.

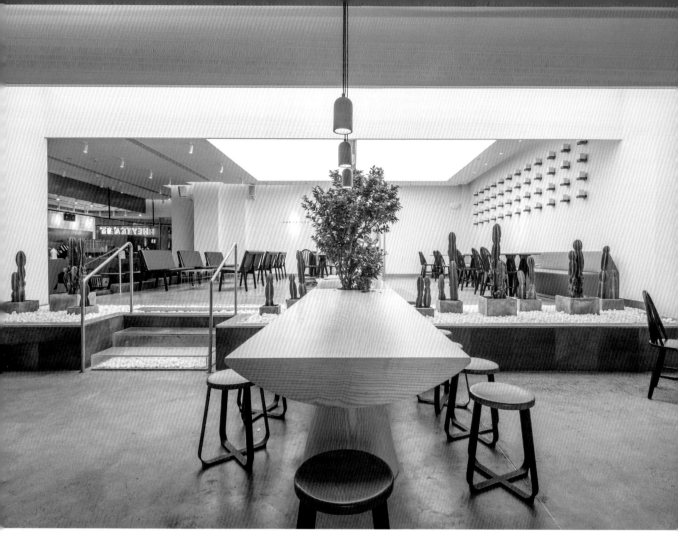

Teasptia

Zones design

Location	Area	Completion	Photography
Wuhan, China	100 square meters	2017	Wang Haibo

Zones design was invited to create a healthy-looking tea space for Teasplia, an original tea brand, following the concept of minimalism and purity. For the layout, the designers opened up two sides of the original irregular façade with the third side of this triangular design providing the service area, thus creating a quiet and attractive interior.

In regard to the décor, the aim was to create a simple space full of appeal. The designers choose various materials, such as white artificial stone, timber, and stainless steel. The long padded bench seating was made a feature on the triangular timber flooring in the center of the space, with the long black bar and wooden furniture adding a masculine edge to this elegant interior. Encased in soundproof glass, the result is a transparent yet quiet tea-drinking space.

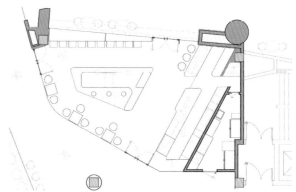

théATRE TEA (Shanghai)

Yen Partnership Architects

Location	Area	Completion	Photography
Shanghai, China	357 square meters	2018	Sui Sicong

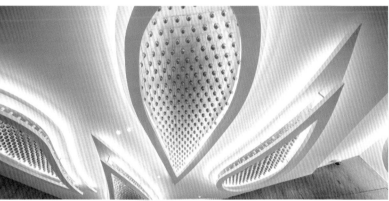

Teahouses have always been perceived as classic or traditional. However, for théATRE TEA in Shanghai, the designers created an ultra-modern expression of the tea culture in everyday life represented through this experimental theatre concept.

The diversity of the tea experience is provided through the retail and tasting area with the form of mixology, as well as bringing tea-making performance, art, and a gallery space into the dining area. Far from the typical tea saloon, here the tea-drinking experience has been being expanded into

a theatrical encounter. There exists a metaphoric rhythm of space that connects each different program together. The designers interpreted the company's motto, "Tea for Life," into a series of spatial languages and aspired to achieve a space to be an ever-evolving experience of the beauty in life.

The venue is a triangular-shaped space with a narrow entrance. The layout concept was to create an internal flow within the space. By utilizing the narrow and deep space, the visual sequence of lighting strip leads the focal point to the tea bar,

which is the stage of this play. As it is a theatrical piece composed of elements—boundaries, a stage, audiences, performers, and a back stage, the designers sought to reinterpret the relationship of "scenes in the play" versus "theater of life" through the design elements.

The Shanghai théATRE TEA is a lifestyle concept store consisting of retail sales, food and beverage, an art gallery, and a multifunction space. The complexity of the program in a limited floor space set the challenge and requirement for the flexibility of boundaries. The designers, therefore, set the movable boundaries and kept the visual connection by using the patterns of the flooring, the steps, and the combinations of furniture.

The program and activity itself also forms a sense of space that sets invisible boundaries. Sometimes the boundaries disappear because of the crossover or mix of the activities. The designers intended to create a rhythm in the space that is an analogy of the traces of tides, and is a boundary at the same time.

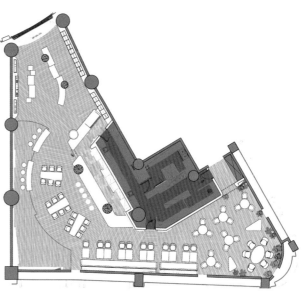

TMB Mixed Tea

DPD Consultant

Location	Area	Completion	Photography
Guangzhou, China	255 square meters	2016	Rui Xukui

TMB Mixed Tea—an acronym of Tea Mixture Bar—is a light, luxury tea brand. Founder Michael Lin, as a designer himself, implemented his own unique style into the design of the store. The style, which is reflected in a black and gold color scheme, used furnishings designed jointly with well-known domestic and foreign brands to condense their own unique brand style.

The overall appearance of the shop is dominantly black to bring out the simple style of the display area, yet was also designed to prevent the main entrance of from feeling too dark or uninspired. The side door is made up of two elements: soft covers and floor paintings. Through the modern design and brand positioning, combined with interesting floor paintings, customers sitting on the sofa or on the side of the bar can admire the paintings.

The concept behind the interior design of the store was to allow the customer to rest comfortably in this predominantly black space. The design team thought about how to enhance the visual and spatial layout for the customer, finally choosing to add gray

hues to break up the space and ensure it was not too monotonous. For the space layout, taking into account the needs of different groups of people, they set up a card area, casual seating, and bar counter, with most of the furniture made of high-end cashmere models, which improved the atmosphere.

The cashier and takeaway areas were positioned in the heart of the store, as it's the primary location to convey brand information and concepts. The cash-register area was designed mainly for displaying information on the products and recent brand activities so that customers can learn more about the brand information. The left side of the dining area was used to display the brand products, serving both a functional and decorative purpose.

An important piece of equipment, the ice machine—used to make many of their specialty drinks—was also displayed to decorative effect, and, to the right, a console and dessert display area completed the design.

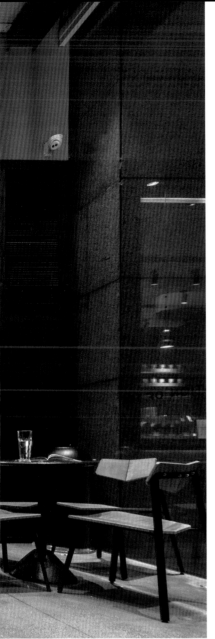

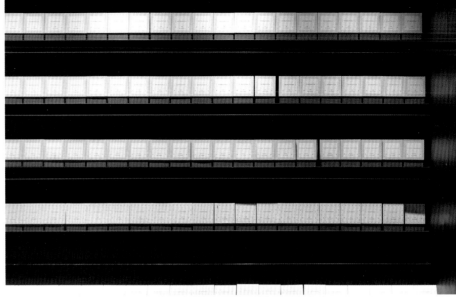

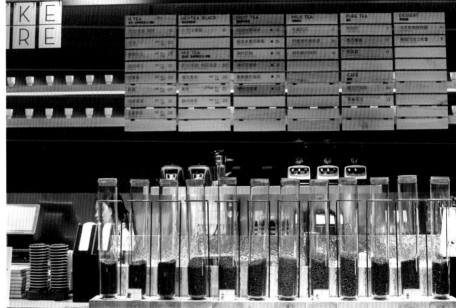

The design of Heytea Black challenged the previous simple style of the white-gray tone of Heytea stores. Its theme sought to highlight fashion taste and elegant style, leading a new lifestyle and consumer trends.

Black evokes elegance and premium quality in the fashion world, and the shop plays with modernity. Situated in a core business building of the city, the aim in the design was to put consumers in a consumption atmosphere of a higher taste and level. The final decision for the site was chosen to be the space beside Prada, which laid the tone for the close relationship between the concept of Heytea Black and fashion and luxury goods.

With "black and gold" as an inspirational element for the store, the design not only inherited the "Modern Zen" style of Heytea, but also used black and gold sustainable materials with a strong sense of the future that agree with modern urban fashion. The two-color combination creates richer spatial layers, giving customers a different multi-dimensional sensory experience for the first time—a sense of grandness and the city.

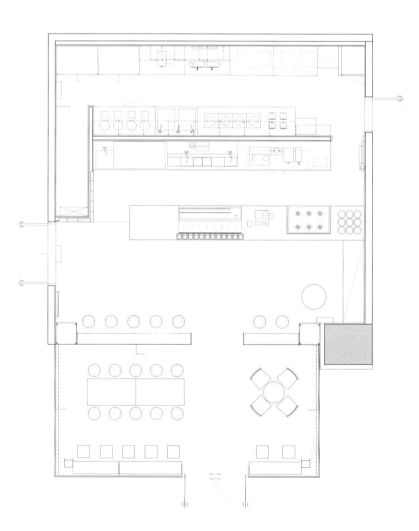

The transparent floor-to-ceiling glass shield, which stands outside the store, wraps the area into a simple, beautiful black space, and segments out a fashionable tea-drinking area facing the street. This unreservedly reveals the concept of extravagance upon entry. Only when one goes through the second door behind the glass shield can they find the main part of the store, where several bar tables are placed in a compact and smart layout.

All tables and chairs in the store were exclusively customized under the theme of "black and gold." The match of white spots with a black base is very trendy. In addition to black long-string cement pendant lamps and spotlights designed for the themed store, lamplights were also especially adjusted to dark gold, creating a sense of fashion and luxury.

Teabank

Crossboundaries (Binke Lenhardt, Dong Hao)

Location	Area	Completion	Photography
Shenzhen, China	1980 square meters	2015	Hao Dong (Crossboundaries)

Crossboundaries designed a field of pentagons for a metropolitan teahouse. A two-floor teahouse of 1980 square meters, Teabank is situated amidst tech corporations and startups in the new Shenzhen Software Industrial Base.

To provide a modern experience of tea—convenience and leisure—Crossboundaries designed the space as both a takeaway and a getaway from the virtual world for tech professionals. The lofty first floor includes a long bar, indoor and outdoor

seating, with ample spaces in the middle for crowds coming from the street and lobby entrances.

Above, an intimate mezzanine and a spatial second floor provide a space for slower-paced activities and events. The second floor consists of a large book collection in its open library, while plenty of seating is spread out for reading and social interactions. Outdoors, a large seating area provides a tea garden and can transform into an event space on warmer days.

Crossboundaries used a pentagon shape to defy the grid layout of the surrounding office towers. When multiplied, the pentagons can be demarcated for either rigid or organic outlines. They propagate like tea trees, taking form as floor, staircase, ceiling, and furniture. The predominant use of wood softens the geometric pentagons and reinforces the sense of earthiness and organic growth that fills the teahouse.

A long, undulating flight of stairs suspends down from the ceiling. It takes the customers from the fast-paced first floor to weave through the steel columns and enjoy the changing atmosphere of the space. As the concrete path continues to the second floor, it is complemented with green woven vinyl that evokes warmth and nature. Enhanced by a hung ceiling and light boxes in the shape of pentagons, this winding journey in Teabank simulates a relaxing stroll through tea fields, giving the customer an experience-focused offline store in the age of ecommerce.

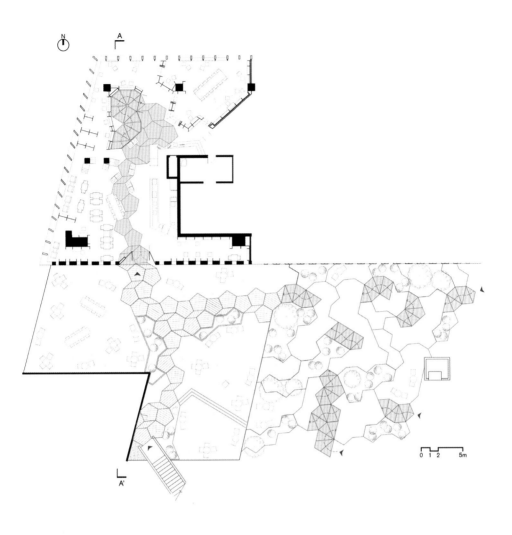

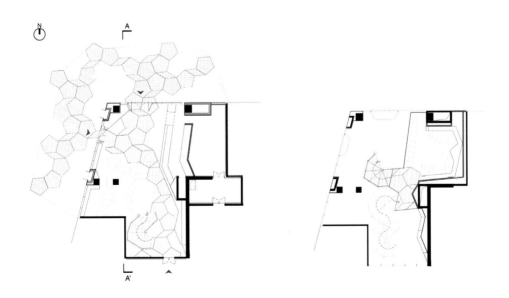

GO FOR TEA

Tang Zhitao / FZD-Studio

Location	Area	Completion	Photography
Foshan, China	195 square meters	2017	Pang Yingshi

The project was commenced in Guangzhou, China in 2017, and came into service in 2018. The life of Canadian cities was the source of inspiration for this store. Brainstorming with the client, FZD-Studio extracted a few key points: forest color, map style, and comfort. By defining the space, the studio introduced a combination of green and rose gold to create a natural and fresh atmosphere.

Tea shops seen everywhere today have developed into social places in cities and GO FOR TEA offers people a relaxing place to enjoy after work.

Based on this positioning, the designer tried to explore the essence of the space through design language, presenting the project in the most natural and light way.

The project attached importance to the space-oriented interactive experience—large open spaces and movable furniture bringing unlimited possibilities for its operation. In addition to enhancing the integrity of the entire public area, the design also satisfied the functional needs of the store, and met the needs of different gathering

occasions and activities, creating a dynamic or relaxed atmosphere.

The designers did a lot of exploration in the use of technology. The square screen wall of spliced wooden strips in green diversifies the partition wall between the front dining area and the service area. For the design of the theme wall, the designer used paintings to decorate the space. As for the front desk, hexagonal bricks and white artificial stone were used in combination to create a simple and clean image.

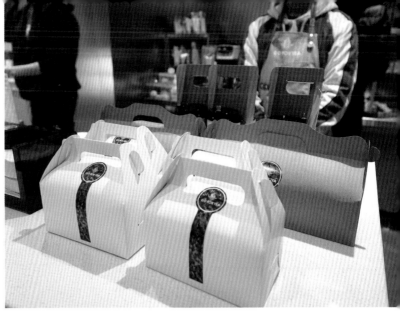

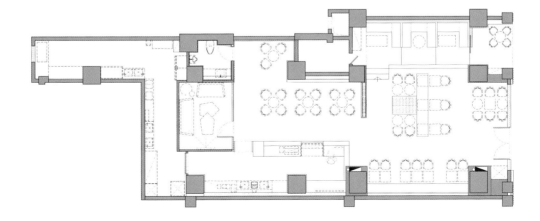

Heytea DP (Uniwalk)

Yan Junjie / A.A.N Architectural Design, MULAND

Location	Area	Completion	Photography
Shenzhen, China	180 square meters	2017	Huang Miangui

To present more designers, brands, and products that uphold the concept of quality and the spirit of the times, Heytea DP (Daydreaming Project) was born. In the DP program, Heytea and independent designers from different fields around the globe conducted cross-border cooperation that is in line with interests of both parties, offering people a more bold and subversive space experience. Heytea DP was the first store included in the Heytea DP program, and in cooperation with architect Yan Junjie, it applied Nordic architectural thoughts in different spaces.

The new store aimed to explore the distance between people in the real world of the new era and a new way for people "sitting down." The designers wanted to conduct an experiment in the space: they put together 19 small tables of different sizes to make a big one, which clears away a sense of enclosure. The big table shortens the distance between different groups and facilitates their interaction.

You can sit opposite each other, back to back, or in a circle. Different ways of sitting down in the same

large space allow the coexistence of both privacy and openness. Consumers can have different spatial experience each time they enter the store.

The encounter was described as "continuous mutual attention between people in public places" and Heytea thinks: Belief gives rise to encounter. Pure white desktops are sleek and simple, and fresh green plants are dotted in the interspaces created by distance, making visual communication between people delicate. The mirror surface overhead reflects real scenes beneath, rendering the overall space bright and open.

In this tea space, you can freely enjoy a rest by themselves, romance between two people, or the joy of a small gathering.

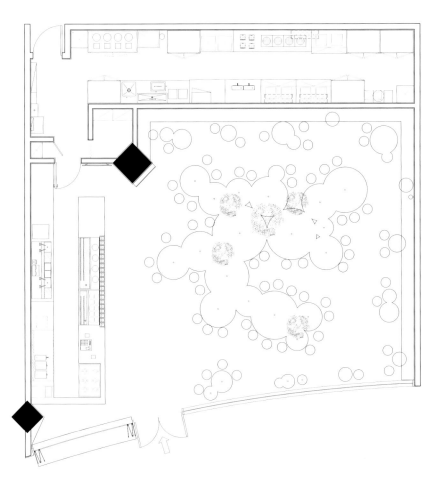

Yue Pao Tea Space

Dao He Interior Design

Location	Area	Completion	Photography
Xinyu, China	144 square meters	2016	Li Di

The design concept of this project was mainly aimed at young adults. A new combination of Chinese art with innovative design techniques, bright modern-art furniture, hand-painted wall art, and stylish lamps made the space vivid. In line with young people's pursuit of artistic personality, this tea shop provides a comfortable space for drinking tea.

The whole theme of youth, calm and steady colors coupled with flexible-personality décor, was articulated with simplicity and windows, making the space more of a mystery. The beauty of life requires

different people to experience it at different times. Nowadays, the era is full of competition; a pleasant space can give you a moment of quiet away from the noise to calm you down and offer a better tomorrow to meet life's challenges.

The spatial solution of the tea bar consisted of cutting its space into "time zones." The curvature of real time zones is generalized in the bar morphology. Each zone begins and terminates with a curve delimiting the spatial area. The shaping of curves creates particular parts of the space, light fixtures,

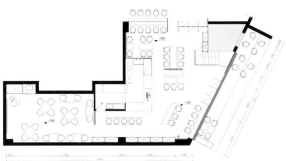

and benches. The space is intentionally unclear, as if blurred, in the same way as the time in which one travels a long distance.

Stainless steel was chosen as the basic material. The bright, subtle steel curves reflect the imaginary lines delimiting the time zones. The shiny metal has associations with both fuselages with riveted sheet metals, as well as the stainless vessels of today's tea.

Heytea DP (Zhongguancun)

MULAND

Location	Area	Completion	Photography
Beijing, China	143 square meters	2018	CAN H

After studying the theme of "interaction between people in a modern space," Heytea DP (Daydreamer Project) continued its journey for new inspiration. This time the designers drew inspiration from the poetic flavor and Buddhist mood of classic Chinese waters and mountains.

The image of the space originates from the painting, *Boat Returning amid Wind and Rain* by artist Dai Jin of the Ming Dynasty and the words of poet Du Fu, "the sound of rain has gradually faded, the air is reflected slightly, and the wind is fluttering like silk."

In the work of Dai Jin, the helmsman in a palm-bark rain cape is poling upstream while fellow villagers on the bridge are walking quickly. The designer brought this artistic conception into this new space and at the same time integrated it with a sense of technology and modernity.

Chinese ink painting differs from Western oil painting. Chinese ink painting expresses the artistic conception of wind and rain in the relations between objects rather than directly describing the form of rain falling from the sky. In the design of the whole space,

Cool
Inspiration
Zen
Design

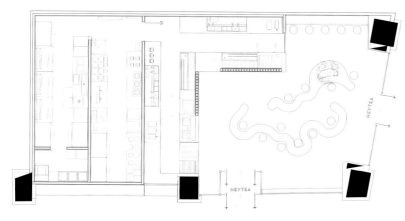

the designer carried on this concept—hundreds of mirrored stainless-steel rods extended at a 45-degree angle from the ceiling, which then stop abruptly in mid-air, thus forming a strong matrix. This element continues until it reaches the bookshelf, commodity shelf, and the showcase outside the door with white aluminum panels as the background.

On the floor of corundum texture, white artificial stones zigzag forward like a shoal in a grand river. The whole space looks leisurely at first glance.

The huge white space is without a stroke of wind and rain, yet evokes a feeling of movement. The mirrored stainless steel turns into reflectors. Therefore, when walking into the space, one can feel the differences of light and shadow due to weather, lighting, and viewing angle inside and outside the room.

The space stimulates the senses and offers new inspiration of deconstruction with a bold and pioneering posture and materials.

Comebuy Tea (Wongtee Plaza)

Hwayon

Location	Area	Completion	Photography
Shenzhen, China	130 square meters	2018	James Chan Studio

The first thing that Comebuy Tea did in Shenzhen was to innovate, thus achieving what it had previously hoped but failed to do. Having gained traction in Taipei, the brand sought to highlight a "zero-distance" concept, being that if everyone is happy to express their differences, the world would be a better place. Additionally, the designers were inspired by the spirit of tea ceremonies and wanted to encourage people to enjoy the experience of talking with each other.

The traditional imagery of tea emphasizes the picture of wandering in mountains, chanting poems, and drinking tea. However, this design sought to subvert the traditional thinking and create a new tea bar focusing on comfort. The whole space combines American iron arts and machinery with oriental bricks and tea. People can enjoy interacting while experiencing the joy of a diversified tea culture. From entering the shop, drinking tea, communicating with each other, then

leaving, consumers can feel the ceremonial aspect of tea culture.

The exclusively designed tea bar allows consumers to experience the fragrance, color, and taste of tea. The busy tea masters who stand in front of the exclusively-designed tea grinders offer a new ritualized sense of tea ceremony. The illustration of a tea extractor on the wall creates a new distance between objects and people, which facilitates the communication between people and tea. The

indoor–outdoor integration, green-plant décor, beams of sunlight, and interconnected seating all promote a welcoming environment for relaxed conversation between people.

Every detail of this space is about the culture of tea, which gradually evolves into the brand culture of the store itself. The collision of passions creates a scene that people can feel in daily life and that is the collision between people and their own inner beings.

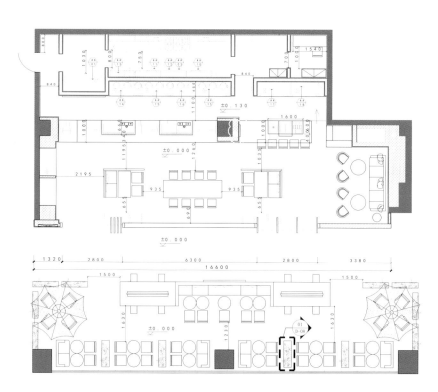

inWE flagship shop (Oriental Plaza)

Young H Design

Location	**Area**	**Completion**	**Photography**
Beijing, China	280 square meters	2017	Xu Feila

It can be a challenge to open a tea shop in Qianmen Street of Beijing as it's easy for people to associate the area with traditional teahouses. As inWE is a modern tea brand, the client wanted to create a completely different experience than that of traditional tea and target the younger demographic.

As such, the designers of Young H Design used a minimalist design to highlight the façade of the flagship store in Oriental Plaza. The shop front is curved to echo the form of the building, while the floor-to-ceiling window reveals the full interior to the passersby with a semi-open façade. The brand murals, which can be seen through the double doors, give consumers a sense of mystery and anticipation.

The front half of the space is open and the latter half is private. At the same time, a hand tea-making bar was introduced to provide more professional tea services. Unlike most tea bars with a completely open design, this project was specially designed with private areas for three to five friends

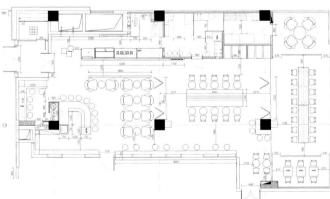

to meet or for business people to negotiate. The space is dominantly blue, and the interior seats are in red, white, and blue—instead of a single color—rendering the entire tea bar more lively and smart. In the space, there is a display area for tea products. This not only serves as advertising and promotion for the brand, but also as an infiltration of tea culture.

The combination of modernity and culture was the original intention of the design. The final shop realized the original concept, which was to the great pleasure of the designers and customers. Both the client and designers aspired to make this a young and energetic space and a new social space for the younger generation in Beijing, enabling them to experience the subtleties of traditional tea culture.

Heytea Pink (Parc Central)

MULAND

Location	**Area**	**Completion**	**Photography**
Guangzhou, China	130 square meters	2017	Huang Miangui

The Heytea team adopted a basic style container and skeleton with restraint for the purpose of making more interesting and bold creations. What is original is that the design theme of Heytea (Parc Central in Guangzhou) starts with color.

It has based its color scheme on the popular Millenium Pink family, a series ranging from pink with light brown to salmon pink with a certain degree of cool gray tone. The color family is a little more vintage than traditional bright pink, and has also been used to great effect in spaces around the world, such as for the façades of Spain's La Muralla Roja apartments in the seaside city of Capel, and the dramatic Paul Smith Pink Wall in Los Angeles, United States. (Moreover, Pantone, the world's most authoritative color research body, opted for Rose Quartz to be color of the year in 2016, a sibling to its 2007 choice, light dogwood pink.)

The use of pink here at Heytea provides a dreamy mist over the space. The designers used a large

number of pink products, such as pink Bang & Olufsen stereos from Denmark, pink birdcage chairs from Philippe Starck, pink Guisset chairs, and pink champagne gold doors.

They also retained tables and chairs of metallic texture, which work as a visual expression of the past, big areas of stainless-steel accessories, and a

buffer space for people to relax. Tea drinkers who seek positive energy and happiness can release the pressure of modern life here. The pink hues can offer tea drinkers a sense of comfort and security.

Human vision is extremely sensitive and critical. Each space has its own story. The trendy and nostalgia pink is cute and willful, like a child.

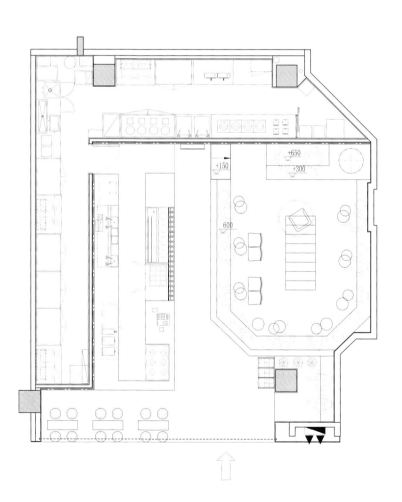

Choui Fong Tea Café

IDIN Architects

Location

Maechan, Thailand

Area

1145 square meters

Completion

2015

Photography

Spaceshift Studio

Choui Fong Tea Café is located in a tea plantation with a number of huge hills. The idea was to keep the hill view where the building rooftop would then be a 360-degree viewpoint of the plantation. Here, at the rooftop, in addition to the natural atmosphere of the plantation, visitors can observe farm activity and tea leaves being hand-picked during the day.

The interior design concept of Choui Fong Tea Café needed to respond to several issues and purposes that were "to create a natural feel, to show a sense of raw materials and especially to be harmonious with the exterior design itself." Therefore, to expose the senses and to create the feel, material selection was an important process and needed to be carefully done. In order to make the materials stand out, the designers chose to make a perceptual contrast. As a result, two materials that were chosen as the main materials of the design were pine and steel. While pine brought a natural feel, steel played an important role in conveying strength and rawness.

To achieve the unity between interior and exterior design, the diagonal wood pattern that was used

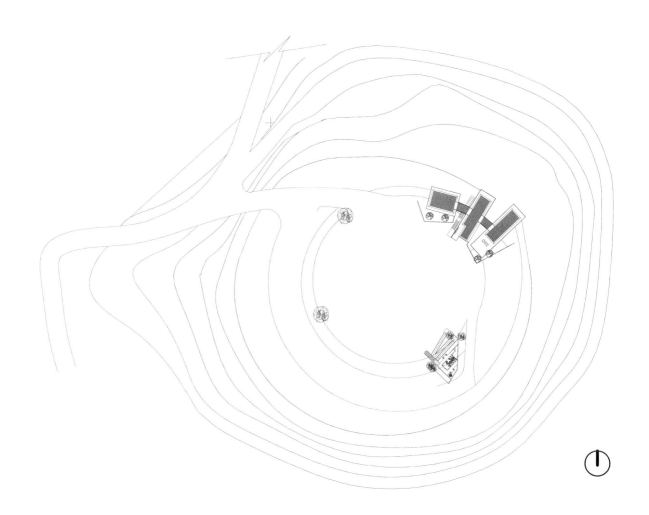

as the exterior feature was also used in the souvenir shop as a pattern in the interior display shelves promoting the recommended items. The two materials, pine and steel, were also used together in the normal product shelves. The shelves display a variety of Choui Fong products, including sweets, tea cups, and particularly their local and authentic tea.

Moreover, using the color black and black steels was another technique used in this interior project to harmonize with the exterior of the café. The pantry counters are also black; the restroom walls were decorated with black perforated steel to create a shade and shadow lighting effect at night.

Apart from the materials use, there is an architectural element that was adopted in the interior design—the table leg. The rectangular diagonal leg stands similarly and identically to the way the columns of the building do.

Taetea Pu'er & Café

Young H design

Location	Area	Completion	Photography
Menghai, China	750 square meters	2016	Xu Rulin

Taetea Pu'er & Café wanted to build its own experience center in the 76-year-old Menghai Tea Factory. The original building was a tea factory built in the 1950s. The client didn't expect a traditional teahouse as it was already well-known among established tea guests. They hoped to create a fashionable new tea-drinking space with its own cultural characteristics to attract young consumers.

With several visits to the original site and discussions with the owner, the design team of Young H design (YHD) added the brand characteristics of Taetea to the original factory culture so as to fully display Taetea's professional study on Pu'er tea and showcase its all-round professional attitude towards Pu'er tea tree planting and consumer service.

The design team narrowed their choice to two daily utensils of the factory—a tea-pressing machine and tea-drying stands, which became the finishing touch of the space. The tea-pressing machine was rebuilt into a retail counter and the tea-drying stands

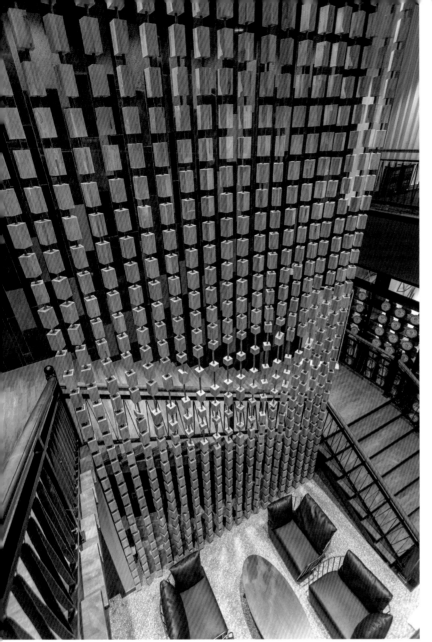

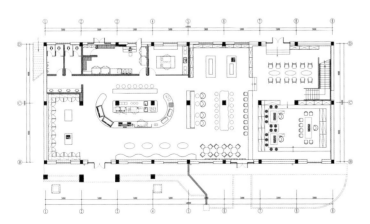

decorate the wall and ceiling. The designers used old wood to represent Pu'er tea's long history, copper to express the color and luster of Pu'er tea, and terrazzo to embody making tea by hand. The two most common materials in tea factories, namely metal and wood, were introduced into the design, rendering a deeper feeling of tea-factory culture in customers.

Taetea Pu'er & Café is an organic combination of tea space and retail space. The 2460-square-foot (750-square-meter) space is divided into a tea-drinking area, a special retail area and a tea-master tasting area. Here, customers can taste a cup of freshly-made Pu'er tea, or buy their favorite tea leaves. From the tea wall and the retail counter remade from a tea-making machine to the "Grand Island Bar" and to the elevated tea-master tasting area, the whole movement line is coherent.

YHD helped a 70-year-old tea brand build a fashionable and modern tea space with rich brand characteristics.

Huishe

Sorabrand

Location	Area	Completion	Photography
Huizhou, China	1600 square meters	2016	Onion, Coff

The return of Chinese aesthetics has always been attributed to the bloodline of Chinese people. The ideal lifestyle of hiding in a city is also the desire of contemporary people. The designers learned about the inheritance and development of Chinese charm, and took the vivid image of "one stroke to the left and another to the right" from traditional oriental culture to form a logo and its extension element, presenting a new Chinese lifestyle.

The package design was inspired by ancient courtyards to reveal the beauty of classic architecture in the action of stretching and opening; the different colors of different packages highlight different qualities of tea. The illustration incorporates ancient ferns with perfect symmetry, echoing the moderate symmetry of Chinese style furniture. The stroke-by-stroke description of the 1000-year-old history of Chinese furniture is an inheritance of Oriental wisdom.

Huishe, as a new Chinese-style cultural life house, is exuberant with the beauty of the East and highlights quality life. The whole space was divided

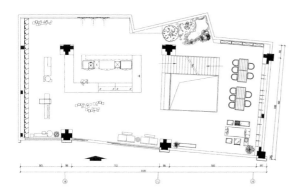

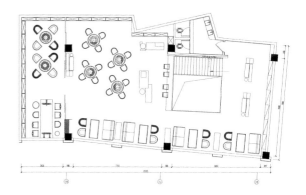

into three-tiers of experience spaces, including Chinese-style furniture and tea sets, light Zen tea rooms, and trending tea drinks. Inspired by "modern life of Oriental aesthetics," the dominating unpolished natural color of the space, simple fence, and casual furniture together create a place of coziness and tranquility.

Huishe is a combination of Chinese and modern design styles. The first floor is divided into a bar area, a retail area of tea-leaves and tea sets, and a small furniture exhibition area. The second floor is mainly a tea-drinking area and an office area. Maple wood is used as the main material to create a relaxed atmosphere. The underground exhibition area is a refinement of traditional Chinese style. While retaining original Chinese tonality, it also incorporates modern design elements. This space is filled with an oriental Zen atmosphere and can satisfy commercial demand, changing the stereotype in people' mind about traditional Chinese cultural home furnishing.

Xiao Guan Tea

Eight Inc.

Location	Area	Completion	Photography
Jinan, China	90 square meters	2016	Wei Xuliang

Tea is one of the world's oldest and most commonly consumed beverages, yet one of the most segmented when it comes to consumer categories. There are two essential categories of tea. There is the common and familiar everyday consumer tea available at local supermarkets, and then there is the unique and specialist tea crafted by well-known tea masters, sold at exquisite prices in rare and hard-to-find boutique shops.

Both categories of tea present their product in similar ways—containers that are exposed to air,

moisture, and other elements, which eventually damages the flavors over time. The flavor of the tea is not well-preserved in either category of tea.

Xiao Guan Tea came into the market with a mission of redefining the way tea is preserved, presented, and consumed in a modern-day context. They used traditional methods to find the best tea in China through mastery and craftsmanship of renowned tea masters combined with technology that allows the peak of the flavor to be frozen in a small capsule—resulting in a product that you can trust.

Xiao Guan Tea solved the dilemma of tea preservation and, with Eight Inc., discovered new ways to differentiate a premium retail experience that would not only redefine how the tea is sold but would also aspire to the modern-day Chinese customer. The designers delved deep into customers' needs and interests to elevate the experience and design a solution that was simple, convenient, self-explanatory, and an honest expression of Xiao Guan

Tea's identity. A modern-day customer might not know everything there is to know about tea, but they have the appreciation for it. Tea enables relationships, and the space needed to express that.

The physical design of the new retail space was inspired by a modernist approach to architecture. The designers wanted to create an open space that had a sense of clarity and purity. Rich bronze

cladding, chrome metal finishes, accents of dark walnut grains, polished concrete floors and ceilings— expressions of modern luxury. Details sampled from luxury car interiors, a comfort of a lounge or a cigar shop—familiar and appreciated by the modern-day Chinese customer.

The experience begins with a captivating storefront that consists of full-height pivot glass doors with product displays creating layers of transparency. An embodiment of trust. The customer is guided through the entrance into the vault. In the vault, tea capsules are displayed on angled shelves along two facing walls in bronze fitted fixtures. Technology was used to create simpler ways of sharing the stories of the tea and tea masters. Stories are activated once the interaction with tea sampling occurs.

Tomás

Savvy Studio

Location	Area	Completion	Photography
Mexico, Mexico	85 square meters	2014	Savvy Studio

Tomás is a teahouse that, through its carefully curated selection, portrays the history, tradition, and culture of the place of origin of each of its products.

The name Tomás makes reference to an important figure in tea's modern history—Thomas Sullivan—who was a New York-based merchant who carefully wrapped tea leaves in individual fabric sachets, patenting thus the first commercial tea bag.

Through a simple and clean identity, the designers portrayed tea itself as an experience—through scent and taste—that translates into wellbeing for body and mind. The design was inspired by the lifestyle that surrounds the daily ritual of drinking tea for which they developed a complex graphic system that helps identify all of Tomás' products, categorizing and emphasizing their origins and key attributes and benefits.

The interior design reinterprets the romantic elements that surround the culture of tea-drinking into a modern setting, using a color palette that

talks about the wide variety of blends the brand has to offer. They communicate a complex ritual, in knowledge and understanding, where each client is invited to create their own environment and their own moment.

The main room is an introduction to both products and scents, featuring each individual tea packaged in large tin containers, unified and coded by the graphic language that was developed. There is a secondary experiential bar where a variety of scents

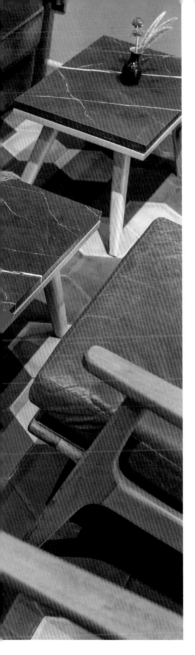

and fragrances can be examined and enjoyed, bringing the consumer closer to the colors and textures of Tomás' tea blends, along with more detailed information about each one and their composition.

A home-like feeling is present in all of the interiors, but more so in the tea room. The furniture was designed by combining materials such as wood, ceramic, and leather, crafted to complement the products' values and functional needs. The walls feature a series of custom, hand-painted illustrations, which portray the concept of tea, in terms of culture, production, and consumption. This, along with a few other vintage elements, communicate a sense of balance between modernity and tradition.

All of the texts were written so that Tomás would turn all of its brand experiences into an actual journey across the emotional—and informational—world of tea, creating, along with its consumers, a new personal story of wellbeing and belonging.

T2 Shoreditch

Landini Associates

Location	Area	Completion	Photography
London, UK	95 square meters	2014	Andrew Meredith

Landini Associates teamed up with iconic Australian tea brand T2 to launch the company's first international store in London. Situated in the heart of Shoreditch's Redchurch Street, the space features a raw, striped-back interior that serves as an antidote to the polished slickness of traditional British teahouses.

Just like T2 itself, the design is dedicated to celebrating the centuries-old art of making and drinking tea. A 98-foot (30-meter) tea library,

housing over 250 different varieties of tea, immerses customers in a knowledge bank of blends from around the globe. At the heart of the store, tea-tasting stations and aroma tables invite customers to stimulate their senses and taste, touch, smell, and compare the different ingredients and fragrances.

Transparent display counters made from layers of interwoven welded steel expose the inner workings of the drawers, from pulls to brass pipes, fittings and sinks. Brewing methods are demonstrated here

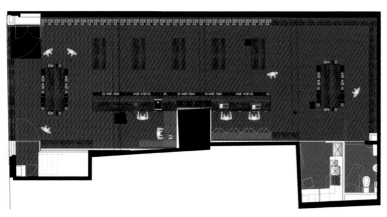

among an extensive variety of tea wares sourced from around the world.

T2's trademark orange packaging is offset by the industrial color palette, most noticeably the blackened, oxidized steel of the tea library. This metal interior extends out onto Redchurch Street and envelopes the front of the store.

While the dark and aromatic design brings a distinctly Melbourne feel to Redchurch street, this new flagship showcases an exciting evolution in T2's store designs. It marks the third successful collaboration between Landini and T2—following the complete redesign of the company's Melbourne headquarters and creation of its brew-bar concept—and preceded the fourth: T2 NYC.

Tea Drop (South Melbourne Market)

Zwei Interiors Architecture

Location	Area	Completion	Photography
Melbourne, Australia	20 square meters	2014	Michael Kai

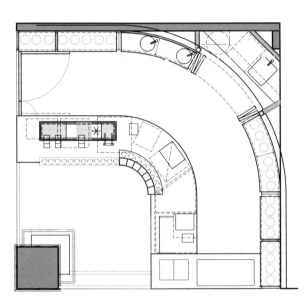

Tea Drop in South Melbourne Market focuses on a sensory tea experience by stripping back the interior, allowing the tea to become the essence of the space. In such a chaotic market site, the space captures the calm and clarity of a modern tea ceremony.

The curved rear wall is used as a device to allow the back-of-house requirements to be concealed from the customer and to position the product as the focal point of the outlet. Lighting focuses the eye on the appealing graded colors on the product display containers and the wall storage solution is used as a feature rather than concealed from view. The counter-line is simple, yet detailed and the materiality and continuity of detail is carried into front-of-house display solutions.

The intent was a restrained retail space allowing the product and brand to be center stage.

Talchá Paulista

studio mk27

Location	Area	Completion	Photography
São Paulo, Brazil	40 square meters	2014	Rômulo Fialdini

Drinking tea was not traditionally a part of Brazilian culture, but globalization and the search for a healthier lifestyle brought with it an increasing interest in tea products in Brazil. Talchá is a pioneer of this new trend, but it is also a result of years of intense studies from the owner, who travelled all around the world in search of a deep understanding of the habit in other countries.

The main goal for the design team was to create a contemporary way of looking at traditional tea salons. At the same time, they wanted to use references from Asian and British culture without looking like an artificial setting, to insert those elements without ignoring the context. Since the site was inside a mall, the space also needed to have cozy mood in a rather aseptic environment.

With an area of 40 square meters, the store is at a corner of the mall. Instead of confining it within glass spans, the choice was to create a wooden lattice that opens entirely as folding panels. The profusion

of light wood and the pendent lights brings a certain
Asian feeling, while the double-height shelves are
reminiscent of traditional British libraries.

0   3m

Ba Lá Trà

The Lab Saigon

Location	Area	Completion	Photography
Ho Chi Minh City, Vietnam	144 square meters	2016	Phong Chac

Ba Lá Trà's owner is a devout Zen Buddhist and tea lover. Her matcha comes straight from Japan, and her Kusmi tea comes from France. The design of the interior is deliberately subtle in order to highlight what is really important in a tea shop: the cup in front of you.

Raw ash wood makes up most of the furniture and fit-out, with polished cement floors for contrast. The designer created options for floor seats as well as table seats. Real rocks dot the space. Buddhist monks were invited to paint scriptures on the wall. The front signage features real grass growing out of concrete crevices. This was achievable by installing a coconut-based mesh and pipe system to control delivery of water to the grass.

The branding contrasts the simplicity of the word mark with the watercolor illustrations of the various fruits and tea leaves that make up Ba Lá Trà's refreshing menu. The color scheme borrows from tea leaves—light brown, deep green, with a neutral beige.

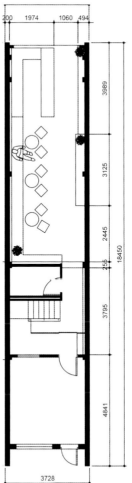

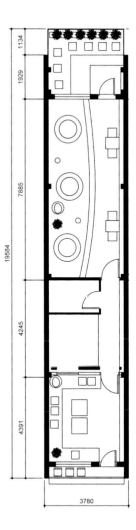

Natural light shines through the two-story façade, with spotlights highlighting each seat. Uniforms are made from canvas fabric, similar to materials that make up tea bags. The staff seemingly blends with the environment.

Branding and interior worked together to complete the experience of creating a space where people can relax and enjoy a cup of tea.

Index

Published in Australia in 2019 by
The Images Publishing Group Pty Ltd
Shanghai Office
ABN 89 059 734 431
6 Bastow Place, Mulgrave, Victoria 3170, Australia
Tel: +61 3 9561 5544 Fax: +61 3 9561 4860
books@imagespublishing.com
www.imagespublishing.com

Copyright © The Images Publishing Group Pty Ltd 2019
The Images Publishing Group Reference Number: 1513

 A catalogue record for this
book is available from the
National Library of Australia

Title: Teatime: Fashionable New Tea Shops
Author: Zender [Ed.]
ISBN: 9781864708325

Printed by Everbest Printing Investment Limited, in Hong Kong/China

IMAGES has included on its website a page for special notices in relation to this and its other
publications. Please visit www.imagespublishing.com